THE BABY ON THE CAR ROOF

and 222 More Urban Legends

THE BABY ON THE CAR ROOF

and 222 More Urban Legends

THOMAS J. CRAUGHWELL

BLACK DOG
& LEVENTHAL
PUBLISHERS
NEW YORK

Published by
Black Dog & Leventhal Publishers, Inc.
151 West 19th Street
New York, NY 10011

Distributed by
Workman Publishing Company
708 Broadway
New York, NY 10003

Designed by Tony Meisel
Book manufactured in Canada
ISBN: 1-57912-147-0

h g f e d

Library of Congress Cataloging -in-Publication Data

Craughwell, Thomas J.. 1956-
        The baby on the car roof and 222 more urban legends / Thomas J. Craughwell.
            p. cm.
        ISBN 1-57912-147-0
        1. Urban folklore—United States. 2. Legends—United States. I. Title.
GR105.5 .C73 2000
398.2'0973'091732—dc21

                                                    00-060790

Contents

INTRODUCTION

You may not have noticed it, but in the summer of 1999 we were all witnesses to the birth of a new urban legend: *The Blair Witch Project*. While urban legends have been the inspiration for plenty of television shows and movies, (the teen slasher film, *Urban Legend*, appropriated at least a dozen), *Blair Witch* was the first time a movie actually fabricated a new UL.

The true-to-life format of the film convinced many viewers that they were witnesses to the real thing. As I stood on line to see *Blair Witch* at my local cineplex, I overheard several people assure each other that we were all about to see a print of the actual videotape found in the Maryland woods a year after Heather, Mike and Josh disappeared. Why did the movie gain such credibility? Because the creators of *Blair Witch* followed the classic four-step formula of a horror urban legend:

1. the characters do something perfectly ordinary.
2. the characters make a simple mistake.
3. the characters become the victims of uncanny events.
4. the characters meet a gruesome death.

The desire to believe that the *Blair Witch* was a true story was so strong among some viewers they were even willing to overlook the fact that Heather and her friends were appearing on talk shows and giving interviews to magazines and newspapers. You really can't blame the movie-going public, however. In a brilliant marketing ploy, a pseudo documentary, *Curse of the Blair Witch*, was released at the same time as the movie and broadcast on the Sci-Fi Channel. *Curse* purports to be an in-depth study of the real-life Blair Witch and the fate of the three unfortunate filmmakers.

Of course, the *Blair Witch* true believers are not alone. Just about every urban legend has its partisans. I've had people tell me that firefighters really did find the body of a scuba diver in the middle of a charred forest in southern California, and that driving around with the car's headlights off is a standard initiation rite of the Latin Kings, and that some poor woman really did think her brains were oozing out of her skull after a canister of cookie dough exploded in her car.

Jan Harold Brunvand, the acknowledged guru of urban legends, has defined the genre as "highly captivating and plausible, but mainly fictional, oral narratives that are widely told as true stories." Plausibility is the key. People have been telling each other vampire stories for centuries, but did you ever meet someone wearing a garlic necklace to ward off the undead? So I have developed my own corollary to Brunvand's definition: we all know that urban legends are not true, except for the one we believe in.

In spite of the *Blair Witch's* popularity, encounters with the supernatural are not the dominant theme in urban legends; paranoia is. In the anxiety-ridden universe of urban legends, carjackers lurk in shopping mall parking lots waiting for female victims to rape and murder; an elderly widow's helpful neighbor actually plans to steal her valuables; a junkie plants a syringe full of heroin in a children's ball pit at a fast food restaurant; a homicidal manic embeds razors in the water slide at an amusement park; and the mysterious deaths of several women is traced back to a rare and deadly spider which made its home in an airport ladies room.

Fear that some foreign and invariably deadly thing will invade our bodies is a staple of urban legends. The heroin syringe in the ball pit is just a spin-off of another urban legend that has been in circulation recently—the AIDS-infected needle that is left in a pay phone coin slot, or jammed into the seat at a movie theater, just waiting for unsuspecting victims to come along and prick and infect themselves.

Why are so many urban legends dark and disturbing? Because they are fun. They deliver a satisfying shiver of fear and excitement, just like Edgar Allen Poe's short stories, or movies like *Jaws* and *The Birds*.

High schools and colleges have always been fertile ground for urban legends. Some of the campus urban legends immortalize local ghost stories, such as the spirits of dead teenagers who spend eternity serving a kind of guard duty at the spot where they were killed, rolling back the cars of other careless drivers who have edged out too far into a dangerous intersection. Other campus-based legends take satisfaction in seeing rough justice meted out to a student who has been behaving badly. A classic example is the story of the mean-spirited college girl who sent her old boyfriend a video of herself doing the nasty with her new lover; the jilted guy gets his revenge by forwarding the film to his ex's parents. And some campus legends are *really* intense cautionary tales, such as the story of the high school girl who took out the family car without permission and caused an accident that killed her boyfriend and her parents.

Which brings us to another popular category: the nobody-gets-away-with-anything urban legends. A shopper who was charged a whopping $250 for a department store's secret cookie recipe exacts her revenge by distributing the recipe far and wide—for free. A wife gets back at her philandering husband by super-gluing his penis to his stomach. When a biker gang humiliates a peaceful truck driver, the trucker doesn't fight back—instead he drives his 16-wheeler over the gang's motorcycles.

At least since the 1940s, celebrities have inspired their own line of urban legends. Some celebrity legends are ironic: for example, the persistent rumor that John Wayne, who played the most red-blooded of Americans, was a draft dodger. Others are a kind of wish fulfillment in which a celebrity with a heart of gold stops to help ordinary folks in a tight spot (The Good Samaritan). Others celebrity legends are about mistaken identity (The Lucky Landscaper and The Bell Hop at the Plaza). Still others try to offer reasons for a star's trademark characteristic (Humphrey Bogart's lisp was the result of a childhood beating, or the result of an attempted jail break, or the result of a wound received in battle during World War II).

Of course, not all urban legends are gruesome. A gentler, kinder urban legend that I heard only a few weeks ago has become my current favorite. It's the story of a would-be archaeologist who thinks he's found an ancient hominid skull, when in fact what he's dug up is he head of a Malibu Barbie.

THE BABY ON THE CAR ROOF AND OTHER AUTOMOTIVE MISHAPS

THE BABY ON THE CAR ROOF

A young couple was driving across the Utah desert. Strapped into a car seat between them was their nine-month-old baby. After seven hours behind the wheel, the husband was beginning to get bleary-eyed.

"You look exhausted," the wife said. "Why don't you let me drive for a while."

"Thanks," the husband answered. "I could use a nap."

He slowed down and parked the car on the shoulder of the highway. The wife climbed out, and lifted the baby in its seat out of the car. "Here," she said, "just scoot over."

"I can't," the husband said. "You've got to move that duffel bag you call a purse out of the way first."

The wife reached up and put the baby on the roof, then reached back into the car and pulled out her large purse. She tossed it into the back seat, walked around the back of the car, and got behind the wheel.

"Sleep as long as you want. I've got everything under control," she said as she put the car in drive.

The wife hadn't driven more than two or three miles down the highway when she heard a siren and in the rear view mirror and saw a state trooper's car behind her with its lights flashing.

"Now what," the groggy husband said.

"I don't get it," the wife said as she pulled over. "What could I have done wrong?"

The state trooper walked slowly up to the car and leaned into the driver's side window.

"Didn't you folks forget something?" he asked.

"Gosh officer," the wife said. "I'm sorry. I forgot to signal before I got back onto the road."

"No," the trooper said. "That's not what I meant."

He straightened up and lifted something off the car roof.

"Actually," he said, "I was referring to this."

He held before the stunned parents' eyes their baby, still strapped into the car seat.

The Elephant and the Volkswagen

Although this story seems to have originated in San Francisco about 1971, the most common version sets it in New York City at Madison Square Garden, the traditional venue for the circus in the Big Apple. The story even appeared in *The New York Times* as a news item in 1975.

A woman from New Jersey drove into Manhattan one morning

to buy tickets for the circus that was appearing at Madison Square Garden. She couldn't believe her luck when she found a parking spot right in front of the Garden. Then, while she was in line at the ticket booth, she saw animal handlers lead one of the circus elephants onto the street for an airing.

"This is such a wonderful day," the woman said to the woman ahead of her in the line. "First a parking spot on the street, and now I get to see an elephant walking on Eighth Avenue!"

The other woman smiled.

"And look," the lady from New Jersey said. "The elephant is walking right over to my car. Oh, I wish I had my camera."

In fact, the elephant was hurrying over to the lady's car. Once it got to the curb, it turned itself around and very slowly sat down on the hood of the Volkswagen.

"You idiot! How could let this happen," she shouted at the handler as she ran to her car.

"I'm really sorry, ma'am." the handler said. "Mambo must have mistaken your Beetle for the red stool she sits on during her act. Come inside with me and we'll straighten this whole thing out."

The woman was still extremely upset, but she followed the handler and Mambo into Madison Square Garden.

The circus' manager couldn't have been more apologetic. He promised that the circus would pay for any repairs not covered by the woman's insurance, and he even gave her a notarized statement describing what happened to her car so she would have no trouble with her insurance company. Then he and the handler followed her back outside to make certain her car was still driveable.

The car may have looked ridiculous with its crushed hood, but because the VW Beetle's engine was in the rear, the car started up without any trouble. Slowly the woman pulled away and headed for the Lincoln Tunnel.

Once she was on the New Jersey Turnpike the woman leaned a little too heavily on the gas pedal. After a few miles, she heard a siren and saw a state trooper's car in her rear view mirror. Stressed and upset almost to the point of tears, she pulled onto the shoulder of the turnpike.

"Ma'am," the state trooper said, "do you know I clocked you doing 85 miles per hour? Let me see your license and registration."

"I know, officer," the woman said. "I'm sorry. I just want to get home."

The state trooper didn't say a word, but walked around to the front of the car to take down the woman's license plate number.

"Ma'am, what happened to your car? Don't you know driving it in this condition is hazardous?"

"Oh, that!" the woman said. "That's from the elephant that sat on my car this morning while I was waiting on line to buy tickets for the circus at Madison Square Garden."

"I see. Step out of the car, ma'am. Can you recite the alphabet backwards for me?"

"I am not drunk! I have a notarized statement signed by the elephant's handler and the manager of the circus!"

"Uh-huh. Good. Before we look at any paperwork, how about you take this breathalyzer test first."

Variant: A St. Louis version has an elephant sit on a family's car in the parking lot of the famous St. Louis Zoo. An English version has the elephant sit on the car when the driver stopped while cruising through a safari park.

The Rattle in the Cadillac

All his life, an insurance agent longed for a Cadillac. After 25 years of hard work during which he built a successful business, bought a nice home for his family, took his wife on an annual vacation to the Caribbean and put his children through college, he decided it was time to indulge himself. He went to a car dealer and bought the finest Cadillac on the market, loaded with every imaginable option.

The day he picked up his new car, the insurance agent was the happiest man in town. The first time he slid behind the wheel of the Cadillac, it was a sensuous experience for him. He ran his hands over the soft leather upholstery. He savored the new-car smell. He sat in the parking lot for a full 10 minutes listening to the low, sexy hum of the engine idling.

Finally, he pulled out of the dealer's lot and drove slowly back to his office about a half mile away.

The excitement of achieving his dream was too much for him, he couldn't get any work done, so the insurance agent took the rest of the day off. He decided he would pick up his wife, take her for a drive in the country, and then they would go have a romantic dinner to celebrate.

As he was heading home, however, he thought he heard a rattle. He tried to ignore it, but there was most definitely a rattling sound coming from his brand-new Cadillac. When he drove over the railroad tracks, the rattling became almost deafening. Now the man was furious. His life-long dream was be ruined by shoddy workmanship.

"Damn American cars!" he said to himself. "I should have bought a BMW."

He turned around and drove the Cadillac back to the dealer. For the next three days, the mechanics at the dealership carefully checked and tightened every single part on the Cadillac. But the car still rattled.

"Take it apart," the insurance agent said. "Disassemble it! Find out what's making that damn noise!"

Later that afternoon, the agent received a phone call from the Cadillac dealer.

"We've found the source of the trouble. Why don't you come over here and take a look."

The insurance agent hurried over to the dealership and into the garage. The entire staff was gathered around his car—the sales team, the mechanics, even the office staff.

"This is it," the owner of the dealership said as he handed the insurance agent a tin can suspended from a string. "We found it hanging inside the door panel on the passenger side of the car. We waited for you to open it up."

The insurance agent took a screwdriver from one of the mechanics and pried open the can. Inside were nuts and bolts, a few pennies, some small stones and a note .

"You rich SOB! So you finally found the rattle!" the note read. It was written on letterhead from the Cadillac factory in Michigan.

Twenty-five Miles Per Hour

In the 1970s this was a very popular story, although its origins almost certainly go back to the 1950s when automatic transmission was a new option.

In 1970, a college kid had bought a used Volkswagen Beetle

with automatic transmission. He was driving to work one morning when his car died in the middle of the street. A few moments later a friend from his fraternity pulled up in his big Chevy Impala.

"What's the trouble," the friend asked.

"The battery's died again," the owner of the Volkswagen said. "I can get it going if you give the car a push."

"I can do that," the friend said.

"There's one hitch," the owner of the Volkswagen said. "I've got automatic transmission. For the battery to kick over, you've got be going 25 miles per hour at least. Can you do that?"

"No problem," the friend said.

"All right," the guy in the Volkswagen yelled over his shoulder. "Start pushing."

Nothing happened.

He looked in his rear view mirror. Half a block away he saw his friend driving his Chevy straight for him at 25 miles per hour.

Cruise Control

In the late 1970s, a man decided to buy an RV for family vacations. One of the options he chose was a new device called cruise control. The salesman at the RV dealership explained that the man could set the speed of the RV and it would remain constant until the driver touched the brake.

The day the man picked up the RV, he decided he'd take it out on the highway to see how it handled. He got the RV up to 60 miles per hour, set the cruise control, and then walked to the back of the RV to get a can of soda from the mini refrigerator.

Meanwhile, the highway curved to the left, but the RV continued cruising straight ahead—at 60 miles per hour—off the highway and into a dense stand of pine trees.

Not long afterward a state trooper pulled up beside the wreck. The man was badly bruised and had suffered a few scrapes, but he was okay. The new RV was totaled.

"I don't understand it," the man said to the cop. "I set the cruise control before I went into the back to get a soda."

"Mister," the cop said, "I think you mistook cruise control for automatic pilot."

Napping in the Nude

A husband and wife decided to drive their RV down to Baja California. After six hours behind the wheel, the husband asked his wife to drive for a while.

"If you don't mind," he said, "I think I'll go in the back and take a nap."

In the back of the RV, the man stripped off all his clothes, stretched out on the bed naked, and fell into a deep sleep.

An hour or so later, the wife heard a rattling sound. She pulled onto the shoulder of the road, got out of the RV, and found the source of the noise: the brace that held the spare gas can to the side of the RV had come loose. A couple turns of the screw and it was secure again.

Meanwhile, the husband woke up. He saw the RV was parked on a deserted stretch of highway. He went up to the driver's cabin, but his wife was not there. He went to the back of the RV and was about to step outside through the back door when he hesitated. Perhaps he should pull on his pants before he went outside.
"The hell with it," he said to himself. "We're in the middle of nowhere." So naked as he was, he stepped outside. But his wife was not in the back of the RV either.

The man was about to climb back inside when the RV pulled back onto the highway. He stood there stunned for just a moment. But even that was too long. By the time he started running after the RV, his wife was cruising along at 50 miles per hour.

The next vehicle that came along the highway was the Mexican highway patrol who arrested the man for indecent exposure.

Spunkball

A group of bored high school boys in rural Illinois came up with a way to generate a little excitement. They invented a game called

Spunkball.

The boys split into two teams. Each team made a dozen "Spunkballs" by soaking rags in gasoline, wrapping the rags in aluminum foil, and duct-taping a firecracker to the exterior of each ball. Then each team got into separate cars and drove around town looking for likely targets.

The object of the game was to find empty parked cars with a window open. Then the boys would light the firecracker and throw the Spunkball into the car. The team that went through its arsenal of Spunkballs first, won.

One team had especially good luck finding parked cars with open windows. In 20 minutes they had tossed 11 Spunkballs. But then their luck ran out. They couldn't find any more targets. Worse, from neighboring streets they could hear explosions and shouts of triumph from their rivals. The opposing team was catching up.

While they sat at a traffic light, the boys argued about which part of town to head to next. Then a car pulled up beside them. Inside was a man and woman and all the car windows were open.

"This is our chance!" shouted the kid who was the keeper of the Spunkballs. He lit the firecracker on the last Spunkball and as the driver gunned the engine, threw it into the neighboring car. The light turned green and as their car raced down the street all the boys hung out the windows shouting "Spunkball!"

They heard the pop of the firecracker and saw a bright flame flare up in the back seat of the car that was still stopped at the intersection. A moment later a huge fireball exploded, destroying the car and killing the passengers.

What's In a Name?

In the late 1960s, General Motors began shipping the Chevy Nova to Mexico. The car had sold well in the United States, it was priced right for the Mexican middle class and GM's marketing department was certain it would be a hit.

After several months in Mexico, not a single Nova had been sold. Back at headquarters, everyone was perplexed. What had gone wrong? The only way to find out was to organize a focus group.

A dozen GM executives flew down to Mexico with one of the best focus group facilitators in the United States. GM's Mexican office found a group of eight men and women who agreed to participate.

On the evening of the focus group, the facilitator showed the eight volunteers the Nova commercials and presented them with the sales brochures.

"Tell me, would you purchase a Chevy Nova?" she asked after she had given the panel a few minutes to review the material.

Everyone around the table laughed.

"Of course not," said a young woman.

"Tell why, specifically," the focus group facilitator said. "Is it the price? Performance? Appearance?"

"You don't understand," a well-dressed man said. "No one here will buy a car that doesn't go."

The facilitator looked confused.

"I'm not following you," she said. "What makes you think a Chevy Nova won't go?"

Everyone in the room laughed again.

"The name gives it away!" the man said. "In Spanish 'no va' means 'it doesn't go.'"

The Accident

A 15-year-old high school girl had just gotten her learner's permit, but her protective parents would not let her use any of the family's cars.

One Saturday night, when her parents had gone out for dinner and a play, the girl went to a party at a friend's house. At the party she met a nice looking soccer player and they decided to go somewhere quiet.

The boy drove to a famous make-out spot. He had brought a bottle of vodka along. After an hour or so he was pretty drunk and pretty obnoxious. The girl announced it was time to go back to the party, and that she was going to drive.

The boy didn't argue, but climbed into the back seat and passed out.

Once she was behind the wheel, the girl realized that her driving skills were not as good as she had thought. Worse, she had never driven at night. They had not gone far before the girl had a serious head-on collision with another car.

When she came to in the hospital, a nurse was standing beside her bed.

"What happened?" the girl asked.

The nurse took her hand.

"It was a very bad accident. The boy in the back seat was killed. So was the couple in the other car. And you were very badly injured. We're doing everything we can for you."

The girl began to cry.

"Please. Please tell my parents that the boy was driving. I'm not allowed to drive. They'll be so angry with me."

"Don't worry," the nurse said. "They'll never find out."

Out in the hallway the nurse met the doctor who was handling the girl's case.

"Did you tell her that she's dying?" the doctor asked.

No," the nurse said. "And I couldn't tell her that the couple in the car were her parents either."

The Body on the Grill

Since 1986, when it was first published in an Ann Landers' column this story has grown in popularity.

After work, a construction worker went out with his friends for a few beers. What began as a couple rounds of drinks turned into an all-night session. It was 2 a.m. when he staggered out of the bar, climbed into his pick-up truck and headed for home.

As he drove through his neighborhood, he felt a bump, but he was took drunk to stop the truck. The man left the truck at the foot of his driveway, stumbled into his house, and passed out on the couch.

The next morning, while he was still in the shower trying to recover from his hang-over, the man's wife was in the kitchen making coffee and listening to the radio. The lead news story was of an eight-year-old from the woman's own neighborhood who had disappeared during the night.

"How terrible," the woman thought. "I'll stop by the house this morning. Maybe the mother needs something." Then she went outside to get the newspaper.

Half-way down the driveway the woman let out a shriek her husband could hear in the shower. He grabbed a towel and ran outside. First, he saw his wife sprawled on the driveway where she had fainted. Then he saw embedded in the grill of his pickup truck, the body of an eight-year-old girl.

The Hook

Everyone in the towns and farms around Joliet, Illinois, were in a state of panic after a serial killer known as "The Hook" escaped from the penitentiary. The murderer had gotten his name after he lost his right hand while making a pipe bomb. Instead of getting a prosthesis, he had replaced his hand with a sharp steel hook—the same hook that he had used to kill 12 young women before he was captured and sentenced to life in prison.

A few days after the killer's escape, a young high school couple were out on a date. After the movie, the boy wanted to go to their favorite spot for a little necking, but the girl refused.

"No," she said. "That lunatic is around here somewhere. Just take me home."

The boy pleaded, and whined, and made exaggerated promises until the girl relented.

"But we're keeping the windows rolled up, the doors locked, and the engine idling," she said.

"You're paranoid," the boy said.

"We do it my way or I go home," the girl answered.

So the boy agreed.

Their private place was the end of a driveway under a huge oak tree on an old abandoned farm. It was far off the road, surrounded by derelict corn fields. No car headlights or even roadside lights reached this dark corner.

The couple had been kissing for only a few minutes when the girl pulled away.

"I heard something," she whispered.

"That's your paranoia again," the boy said. He kissed her and the girl returned his kiss, but her heart was not in it. Again she pulled away.

"You had to hear that scratching sound," she said.

"No," the boy said. "I didn't hear anything." He tried to take his girlfriend in his arms again, but this time he stopped. He did hear a scratching sound against the passenger side door of the car.

"It's him!" the girl whispered.

"It's that huge raspberry bush," the boy said.

"Get me out of here," the girl said.

The boy started to protest, but the scratching sound was louder and more distinct than ever now.

"Go! Go now!" the girl shrieked.

The boy threw the car into drive and hit the gas. The car lurched forward down the old driveway, spewing gravel and dust behind it.

All the way home the girl wept from fright. When he boy pulled up in front of her house, he got out and walked around to open her door and help her out of the car. He reached for the handle then yelled, jumped backward, tripped over his feet and fell flat on his back.

The girl threw open the door.

"What is it? What's wrong?"

"Look! Look!"

Hanging from the car handle was a bloody hook.

"No Radio"

A woman who lived in New York City had a car but couldn't afford the $250 a month to park it in a garage. That meant her car was out on the street, prey to car thieves and vandals. She could deal with getting up in the morning to find her car tagged by graffiti artists, but having a window smashed and her radio stolen time and again was maddening.

Finally, after the fifth radio had been ripped out of the dashboard, the woman went to her mechanic and told him to tape up the exposed wires and not bother putting in a new sound system. That night, when she parked the car on the street, she placed in the windshield a large sign that read "NO RADIO!"

The next morning she went outside to find the driver side window smashed. Taped to the dashboard was a sign that read "JUST CHECKING."

A Tale from the Tollbooth

Two Goths took the New Jersey Turnpike to their college in

Newark. Every day the stopped at the same tollbooth. Every day they asked the collector, "How much?" And every day they got the same answer. "Seventy-five cents, boys. Just like yesterday."

As pranks went, this was pretty dull. Even the tollbooth collector was bored with it. Then one of the boys had an idea that would make their next trip down the Turnpike memorable.

The next morning, the Goths pulled up to their usual tollbooth and asked their usual question.

"How much?"

"Same as yesterday," the collector said. "Seventy-five cents."

"That's a rip-off," the driver said. When he reached out his window, instead of dropping three quarters into the collectors outstretched hand, he clamped a handcuff around the man's wrist.

"What the hell are you doing?" the man said. And then the collector noticed that a rope was tied to the other cuff.

The driver gunned the engine and shot out of the tollbooth. As the rope uncoiled out the car window, the collector screamed and tugged at the cuff, trying to free his hand. It wouldn't come off. His arm was going to be ripped out of its socket. The poor man began to weep.

Then he saw the frayed end of the rope flutter out of the car window.

300 Miles to the Gallon

In an effort to recapture the United States automobile market, an American car maker developed an engine that could run for 400 miles on one gallon of gasoline. The remarkable new engine was placed in a dozen cars and these test models were sent out to dealers across the United States with instructions to road test the cars under the greatest variety of driving conditions.

A dealer in Minnesota received one of the experimental cars. Aside from its color—a metallic mint green—it looked like every other four-door sedan on the lot.

Not long after the experimental car arrived, an elderly woman came to the dealership to pick up her new sedan. She had special ordered her car in metallic mint green. The salesman went into the front office to get the new keys, grabbed the keys for the experimental car by mistake and escorted the lady out onto the lot. There, side by side, were two identical metallic mint green sedans.

The salesman tried the keys on one, but the door wouldn't unlock.

"Then this one must be yours, ma'am," he said as he unlocked the experimental car and held the door open for the customer.

She thanked him, took the keys, fired up the ignition and drove away.

For the next week, no one at the dealership had a spare moment to road test the experimental car. At the end of the week, the elderly lady came into the showroom looking very unhappy. Her salesman was out to lunch so the dealer himself asked if he could help her.

"The car handles beautifully," she said. "But the gas gauge is broken."

"How do you mean 'broken'?" the dealer asked her.

"I've driven more than 300 miles since I picked the car up last week, and the gas gauge hasn't moved a bit. Can your service people repair it?"

The dealer was stunned. He couldn't say a word.

"I don't want to make trouble," the woman said. "I saw another metallic mint green sedan on your lot last week. Would it be too much trouble to just trade my car for that one?"

The car dealer swallowed hard.

"No trouble at all. I'll make the trade right now. And I'll refund you half the purchase price of the car for your trouble. Just take a seat here. I'm going to pull your old car into the garage so it won't be sold by mistake to any other customer."

The Security System

A mid-life crisis hit a quiet, timid antique dealer in an odd way. He went out and bought a cherry red Alfa Romeo sports car.

The man loved his new car. When he raced it down the highway, he didn't feel middle-aged and prudent—he was young and hip. But after a few weeks the man began to worry. What if his car was stolen? It wasn't just a possession, it was now a vital part of his identity. He couldn't bear the thought of someone, undoubtedly younger and cooler than he, stealing his sports car.

So the antique dealer hired a contractor to tear down his old wooden garage and build a new one out of cinderblock with a reinforced concrete roof and no windows. It looked like a bunker, but that was only the beginning. Then he had a home-security service come in and install their finest alarm system. Finally, he bought the heaviest chain he could find and the most secure locks. Each night he chained the frame of the Alfa Romeo to bolts in the garage floor, set the alarm, locked the garage and went to bed.

At last, the antique dealer felt confident that his sports car was safe. Even a rash of car thefts in his neighborhood did not concern him.

One morning he opened his garage door and was stunned by what he saw. His beloved Alfa Romeo was still there, completely unharmed, but someone had turned the car around 180 degrees! And taped to the windshield was a note that read, "When we want it, we'll come and get it."

The Deadly Airbag

This story is the most recent of airbags-can-be-lethal folklore.

A man driving on Route 80 in Ohio stopped at a rest stop to use the men's room and get something to eat. When he returned to his car, he found that he locked the keys inside. Angry and embarrassed, he pulled out his cell phone and called the cops for help.

A few minutes later a highway patrol car pulled up. The officer took a metal rod he called "a slim jim" out of the trunk and slid it between the door window and the frame to unlock the car. After several attempts, the cop still hadn't hit the mechanism that controls the door lock release. Impatient and frustrated, the state trooper jammed the rod down hard, it slipped out of his hand, and struck the airbag panel in the steering wheel.

When the airbag inflated. The force propelled the rod out of the car and into the state trooper's skull. By the time the ambulance arrived he was dead.

The Exploding Cellphone

All versions of this urban legend can be traced back to Southeast Asia. Nonetheless, the story is so widespread in the United States that National Public Radio devoted a segment to it.

An executive was late for a meeting in downtown Los Angeles. As he sped along the freeway, he noticed that he was almost out of gas. Cursing furiously, he got off at the next exit and pulled into a gas station. He leapt out of his car, and jammed the nozzle into the gas tank.

"Damn! I'll never get there on time," he said to himself. So he reached into the car, opened his brief case, and took out his cellphone.

"Maybe I can get them to postpone the meeting for half an hour," he said.

The executive flipped open his phone and dialed the client's number. The spark from within the cellphone ignited the gas fumes, then the car's gas tank. A huge fireball engulfed the executive, followed by an explosion that leveled the gas station.

The Slasher Under the Car

A single woman bought a small house in a college town. After a couple of days, one of her neighbors dropped by to welcome her to the neighborhood.

"Forgive me for asking," the neighbor said, "but do you have hiking boots?"

The newcomer thought it was an odd question. "No. Why do you ask? Are you a hiker?"

"Me? No way," the neighbor said, and laughed. "I hate walking anywhere. I'll drive around a parking lot for 15 minutes to find the closest spot to the mall door. And that is really my point. You see, we have some trouble here with the frat boys."

The newcomer poured her new friend another cup of coffee.

"One of the frat houses has a notorious shoe fetish. And the way the boys add to their collection is not nice. At night, they send pledges out to the mall parking lots. The boys lay underneath cars and wait for women wearing fine shoes to walk by. Then they reach out and slash the woman's ankle with a knife. While she's lying on the ground yelling, they steal her shoes and run back to the frat house."

"That's sick!" the newcomer said. "Has it happened to you?"

"Only once," the neighbor said. "I lost a $300 pair of Prada shoes. But now whenever I go shopping I wear heavy, ugly hiking boots that go halfway up my calf. And the frat boys keep their distance."

The Rest Stop

One summer a family from Maine decided to visit relatives in Arizona. The mother and father thought the visit would be a more memorable experience for their three children if they drove rather than flew. Initially, the trip was exciting, but day after day in the car made the children cranky.

There was one day when the children were just impossible. The family had been on the road for a week. It was hot. The drive through West Texas was boring. The kids were fighting constantly in the back seat.

"Just pull over somewhere," the mother said. "Maybe if we give them something to eat and let them run around for an hour they'll take a nap and we can get some peace."

Up ahead the father saw what appeared to be an exit. "Maybe there will be something there."

He turned onto the ramp, but the exit led nowhere. The pavement ended abruptly and there was nothing but the endless plain.

"This is weird," the father said. "Whether they were planning an exit or a rest stop, the highway department must have abandoned the idea."

"I don't care about the reason," the mother said. "I'm just happy to get off the road for a while."

The father parked car at the end of the pavement, and the mother laid out a blanket on the grass where the car provided a little shade.

While the family of travelers was eating lunch, back on the highway an 18-wheeler was in trouble. The truck's brakes were gone, and the trucker was desperate to find some grassy place where he could get off the road safely and just let the truck lose its momentum. Then he remembered the abandoned exit just up ahead.

The 18-wheeler was speeding along at 60 miles per hour when

it began its descent down the ramp. The trucker saw the car parked dead ahead. He leaned on his horn. The low blaring sound was the last thing the family heard before the truck smashed through their car and crushed them all.

The Carjacker I

After a full day of Christmas shopping at a mall, a woman returned to the parking lot just in time to see a man climb into her Mercedes.

"Stop! she cried. "Get away from that car!"

The man looked at her with contempt.

"Get out of my way, lady," he said.

The angry woman dropped her shopping bags, opened her purse and took out a hand gun.

"Get out of that car or I'll shoot!" she said.

"You're out of your mind," the man said as he climbed out of the car and started to walk toward the woman. Before she knew what she was doing, the woman pulled the trigger and shot the man in the leg.

"You are insane!" the man screamed. Clutching his wounded leg, he dragged himself away and hid under one of the neighboring cars.

Frightened and afraid that she would be arrested, the woman threw all her packages into the back seat of the car and climbed in behind the steering wheel and she realized this was not her car.

The Carjacker II

A young woman was driving home in her 4x4 one evening when she saw the body of a man lying in the road up ahead of her. She slowed down, but realizing that this was a ploy carjackers often used, she decided to play it safe. She drove off the road, through the underbrush and then returned to the highway again.

"Of course," she thought to herself, "it might actually be someone who needs help." To be on the safe side, she drove to the nearest police station and reported the incident.

When the cops got to the scene, there was no body lying in the road. There were, however, the bodies of four armed men lying in the underbrush. The woman had driven over them when she made her detour.

THE RHINO AND THE CRAZY GLUE AND OTHER ANIMAL STORIES

THE RHINO AND THE CRAZY GLUE

A man just out of college was visiting a petting zoo with his girlfriend when another couple approached him. They spoke a language that sounded like Russian, and the woman had a tube of Crazy Glue in her hand. She asked the American a question which, of course, he didn't understand, and pantomimed applying the glue to her lips.

"Oh gosh, no!" the man said. "That stuff's not for chapped lips. It's Crazy Glue. It's super sticky stuff. Here, watch."

The American took the tube of Crazy Glue from the woman, applied a generous amount to his hands, and then put his hands on the posterior of Sally, a tame adult rhino that was part of the petting zoo.

"See! The rhino can't go anywhere now. This glue sticks like crazy!"

The Russian tourists clustered around the rhino's posterior to admire the adhesive qualities of Crazy Glue, but all this attention to her hindquarters made Sally nervous. She decided to trot over to the far side of the petting zoo enclosure. Naturally, she took the helpful American with her.

Now Sally was getting upset. No matter where she went or how fast she turned, she couldn't shake the human off her butt. Sally panicked and ran wildly around the enclosure. The other animals became terrified, too, and started a stampede.

In her frenzy, Sally chased all the visitors out of the enclosure, destroyed a concession stand, and trampled three miniature goats, a Vietnamese pig, and a small flock of ducks. She only stopped when a zoo caretaker shot her with tranquilizer gun.

Sally collapsed on the ground, and the terrified, exhausted nimrod who had glued himself to the rhino's buttocks collapsed behind her. But the trouble didn't end there. A few moments after the rhino collapsed, the laxative the zoo's vet had given Sally earlier in the day went into action.

Thirty gallons of rhino dung erupted out of Sally and all over the hapless American. While two of the zoo's maintenance crews worked with shovels to clear away the dung so the poor man could breathe, one of the zoo's vets applied one solvent after another, trying to find something that would detach the man's hands from Sally's rear end. After an hour of effort, the man was free.

Gasping for air and gagging from the stench of the rhino dung that covered him from head to foot, the man staggered out of the petting zoo enclosure. At the gate stood the two Russian tourists and an elderly woman who was laughing and chatting with them in Russian.

"They want to thank you for the performance. They say you are better than the clowns in the Moscow Circus, and they want to know what time is your next show," she said in Russian-accented English.

The SUV on Ice

After a major score in the stock market, an investor from Detroit went out and bought himself a $50,000 Grand Cherokee. This SUV was loaded, and the guy was pretty proud of himself. So to show it off, he invited a friend to go duck hunting.

Early the next Saturday morning they loaded the guns, the beer, and the investor's labrador retriever into the Grand Cherokee and headed north to duck country.

It was late in the season, so their favorite lake was frozen solid, which gave the proud SUV owner an opportunity to drive his new baby out on the ice.

"Your Cherokee handles beautifully on ice, Eddie," the friend said, "but how are we gonna attract ducks? They only land on water, and we don't have any tools to cut a big enough hole in the ice."

"Sure we do," Eddie said. He climbed out and walked to the back of the SUV, followed by his friend and his retriever. Eddie opened his tool chest and took out a stick of dynamite with a 40-second fuse. "This should make a nice big hole in the ice," he said. "You light the fuse and I'll throw the dynamite."

As the fuse began to sizzle, Eddie put everything he had into the throw. The stick of dynamite soared high over the ice and landed far out on the lake. And as the stick of dynamite bounced on the ice, Eddie's lab took off like a shot to retrieve it.

Now both of the men are screaming at the dog.

"No! Stop! Come!"

But the lab was a dog with a purpose. He picked up the stick of dynamite, tossed his head back, and started prancing across the ice back toward the two hunters.

The two men are almost hysterical now.

"Down! Sit! Stay! Heel, dammit!"

But the dog and the dynamite kept coming.

Desperate, Eddie ran to the back of his SUV, took out his gun, and shot his dog.

Now the gun was loaded with bird shot, which will bring down a duck; it won't stop a 100-pound dog, but it will slow him down. The lab hesitated for a moment, but then kept walking toward his master.

Eddie fired again, and now the dog, hurt, confused, and frightened, looked for some place to hide. With the dynamite still in his mouth the lab took cover—underneath the Grand Cherokee.

As the two hunters scrambled to get away, the dynamite exploded, a huge hole opened up in the ice, and the Grand Cherokee sank to the bottom of the lake.

The two men were silent for several long minutes. Then the friend spoke up.

"So Eddie, you think your insurance will cover this?"

The Choking Doberman

This story dates at least from the 16th century. One peculiar modern version concludes with the vet telling the dog owner that the dog will have to be destroyed because once it has tasted human blood it will be a killer for the rest of its life.

A woman came home very late one evening to find her Doberman Pinscher lying on the living room floor, blood coming from its mouth, and choking. She called her vet who told her to bring the dog to the animal hospital at once.

In the examination room the vet gave her initial diagnosis.

"Whatever your dog tried to swallow is still lodged in its throat," the vet said. "And from the blood I'd say that whatever is down there has ruptured a blood vessel. I'll have to operate. Why don't you go home, and I'll call you in a couple of hours after surgery."

When the woman entered her house, she was surprised to hear her phone ringing. The vet couldn't have finished the operation already. She barely had time to say hello when she heard the vet shouting.

"Get out of your house now! Use your cell phone, call the police, and tell them you have an intruder. I'll meet you in front of your house in a few minutes," he said.

The poor woman was startled, even frightened, but she did as she was told. She ran out of the house and down the street where she called 911 on her cell phone. A few moments later two cops and the vet pulled up in front of the house.

"Did you call about a break-in, ma'am?" one of the cops asked.

"Yes," she said, "but I don't know anything about it. You'll have to talk to my veterinarian."

The two cops exchanged dubious looks, but the vet spoke up.

"It's like this officers. This lady found her dog choking to death tonight. When I examined the animal's throat I found these." From her coat pocket the vet drew out a clear plastic bag. Inside were three human fingers.

"It seems to me that the intruder could still be inside the house," the vet said.

"We get the picture," one of the cops said. "Both of you wait here while we search the house."

A few minutes later the police officers emerged from the house. They had a man with them, who was moaning and clutching his left hand which was covered with blood and missing three fingers.

The Hare Dryer

A man opened his back door one Monday morning to find his dog proudly holding a piece of dirty fur in its mouth. Upon closer inspection, the man was horrified to see that the dirty fur was actually his neighbor's prize rabbit.

He got the rabbit away from the dog and carried it into the house. The animal was dead, but there was no blood, no puncture wounds. "The damned dog must have broken the bunny's neck," the man thought. And then he had an idea.

He carried the rabbit to the bathroom, placed it in the tub, and grabbed the bottle of shampoo. He washed away all the dirt, used a little conditioner to make the rabbit's fur shine, and blow dried it.

Then, after reassuring himself that his neighbor was not home, he ran across the yard, placed the rabbit inside its hutch, and scurried back to his own house.

A few days later the man ran into his neighbor. "The strangest thing happened," the neighbor said. "I found my rabbit dead in its hutch Monday morning."

"I'm sorry to hear that," the man said. "It must have been a shock."

"It was a shock," the neighbor said. "Because the rabbit died over the weekend and I buried it Sunday."

The Bump in the Rug

Three carpet installers pulled up in front of a house in suburban Illinois where they were scheduled to lay wall-to-wall carpeting on the first floor. The lady of the house met them on the porch with her seven-year-old daughter.

"I have some errands to run this morning," she told the men. "I should be back in two hours."

"That's fine," the foreman said. "We'll be finishing up by then."

The woman and her little girl went off on their errands and the men went inside the house and got down to business.

It was a simple installation job. The crew finished in a little over an hour, so they sprawled out on the new carpet and relaxed until the woman returned. Then the foreman noticed something.

"Damn it! Look at the bump in the corner."

"It's not a big deal, boss," one of the men said. "I'll just tear up the corner and recut it."

The foreman glanced out the window and saw the woman's car pulling into the driveway. "She's home. Just take a hammer and pound that thing out."

After a couple of forceful blows of the hammer, the bump was flat. And a moment later the mother and daughter came through the front door.

"Mommy, I want to play with my hamster," the little girl said.

"You go ahead, sweetheart. I have to talk with these nice men."

The woman was delighted with her new carpet and that the men had finished the job so quickly. While she was writing them a check, the daughter came out of her bedroom crying.

"Mommy, the hamster's gone. The cage door is open and he's gone!"

The mother picked up her daughter and kissed her forehead. "These nice men are about to go, then you and I will look for the hamster. Okay?"

"I don't suppose you saw a hamster around while you were laying the carpet?" the woman said to the carpet installers.

The three men looked at each other, then glanced over to the corner. Where the bump in rug had been there was a now a fresh, wet, little puddle of blood.

Don't Leave Home Without Her

A Swiss couple from Zurich had no children, but they did have a poodle they were extremely fond of. They never went anywhere without their little dog, so when they planned a vacation to Hong Kong naturally they brought little Fritzie with them.

Their first night in Hong Kong they decided to dine out at a restaurant down by the harbor. As usual, they took the poodle with them. When their waiter came to their table, the woman handed her dog to him.

"While we have dinner, please take Fritzie to the kitchen and give him something to eat," she said.

The waiter did not speak much German. He looked at the couple strangely and was reluctant to take the dog from the woman's arms.

"It's alright," she said, "just take him to the kitchen."

. The waiter shrugged, took the dog and walked away. Then he returned for the couple's order.

The travelers were ecstatic as course after course of delicious Chinese cuisine came to their table. Then the waiter emerged from the kitchen and rolled a cart bearing a large covered tray up to the Swiss couple's table.

He smiled warmly.

"I did as you asked," he said, then he lifted the cover. Lying on the tray surrounded by beautifully carved Chinese vegetables was little Fritzie, roasted to perfection.

Fetch!

Truman Capote is said to have told this story when he was a guest on The Johnny Carson Show.

A young man went to pick up his new girlfriend at her place on the twenty-third floor of an apartment tower on Manhattan's Upper East Side.

"I'm not ready to go yet," she said as she escorted him into the living room. "Have a seat. I only need a couple more minutes. You can get acquainted with my dog. He likes to play fetch."

Beside the couch was a pink rubber ball. The young man bounced it a few times off the floor, while the dog, a friendly little terrier, jumped up and down and yapped with excitement.

"Okay pooch, we'll start with something easy."

The young man tossed the ball against a bookcase. The dog caught it on the rebound in mid air.

"Good boy! Try this one."

The young man threw ball against the far wall of the living room. Again the terrier snatched the ball out of the air and brought it back to the boyfriend.

"Okay, dog, show me what you've got." Now the young men threw the ball hard so that it bounced at the threshold of the French doors that opened on to the balcony.

The terrier dashed across the room after ball, made a beautiful leap into the air, snatched the ball, and with it still in its teeth, sailed over the balcony railing.

Kitty's Place in the Sun

A New Yorker had a cat that he treated as the most important thing in his life. In spite of years of pampering, the cat became arthritic in its old age. The cat's owner couldn't bear the sight of his pet stiff and uncomfortable, so he made a drastic decision. He quit his job, sold his penthouse on the Upper East Side, and bought a house on the edge of the desert in Arizona. The man was certain his cat would be more comfortable in the warm, dry climate.

The morning after they moved into their new home, the man opened the sliding glass doors and carried his old cat onto the sun-drenched patio. He placed the cat on its favorite blanket dead center on the terrace and then went back into the house to make coffee.

As the cat stretched out in the sun, the man felt certain that he had done the right thing. By moving to Arizona he was sure that he had added years to his beloved kitty's life.

At that moment, a shadow circled the patio. Suddenly a large eagle pounced, lifted the cat in its talons, and carried it away.
Variant: A related version of this story has tourists traveling with their poodle to an aquarium. At the shark tank, the tourists toss a hot dog into the water. Their poodle dives in after it and is eaten by the sharks.

"Bad Fifi!"

A wealthy couple in Miami hired an interior decorator to redecorate their apartment. It was a painless job—the clients were easy to please, had lots of money to spend, and stayed out of the decorator's way. The only trouble was the couple's obnoxious toy poodle, Fifi.

The dog followed the decorator wherever he went, yapping at him constantly, and running off with any tool or fabric swatch that he happened to put down. Not a day went by that the little mutt didn't sneak up from behind and bite the decorator in the ankle.

After weeks of this, the job was nearly complete. The husband and wife were sunning themselves on their deck while the decorator was going around the living room with a can of paint and a small brush doing touch-up work. Suddenly, he tripped and spilled the entire can of paint on the new $10,000 Persian silk carpet. The decorator was mortified to be so clumsy. But the thought of having to pay for another $10,000 carpet out of his pocket was what really upset him.

In the corner of the room was Fifi, yapping and snarling as usual. That's when the decorator had an idea. He reached into his pocket and took out a mint. Holding it in the palm of his hand, he got down on his knees. "Come here, Fifi. Come get the candy, sweetheart!"

The dog scampered across the room, and as it took the mint, the decorator grabbed him by the scruff of the neck and rolled the dog in the spilled paint.

"Oh, Fifi!" he shouted, loud enough so his clients would hear him. "Look what you've done!"

The Greenhorn

Stories of city slickers who can't tell the difference between wildlife and farm animals go back centuries. One modern version tells of farmers who paint "COW" and "HORSE" on the side of their animals for the benefit of clueless hunters from the big city.

A man from Manhattan who had never been outside New York City dreamed of the rugged life on the range. When he reached his forties, the man decided to act on his life-long dream. He bought an expensive hunting rifle and signed up for shooting lessons at a posh rifle club. After several months of practice, he felt he was ready to go hunting. At the beginning of the hunting season, he bought a first class ticket to Wyoming, rented a Jeep Cherokee at the airport, and drove up into the mountains.

He stopped at the first ranch house he saw and asked the owner if he could hunt on his land.

"That's fine with me," the rancher said. "Only watch out for my bull. It's grazing in the upper pasture, and if you shoot it, it will cost you $5000."

The novice hunter promised to be careful.

A couple hours later the hunter stood at the rancher's door again. "I'm terribly sorry," he said. "In spite of everything you told me, I mistook your bull for an elk and shot it. Will you accept a check?"

The rancher was angry, but at least he would be compensated

for his loss. He took the New Yorker's check for $5,000 and watched him as he drove back to the main road. Then the rancher called one of his hands from the barn.

"That New York hunter shot the bull. Help collect the body and we'll have steaks tonight."

In the upper pasture, the two cowboys were surprised to see the bull grazing quietly amid the tall grass.

"What in hell did that city boy shoot?" the rancher said. As they wandered around the field, the ranch hand found the body of a magnificent eight-point buck.

"This is some day for you, boss," the hand said. "You've got a trophy buck, a freezer full of fresh venison and a $5,000 check."

"Yep," the rancher said. "I got to figure out a way to get more New York hunters up here."

The Deer Hunter

Every year for twenty-five years a Wisconsin man had gone deer hunting. Every year he bagged a deer. Still, he wasn't satisfied. Of all his friends, he alone had never shot a trophy buck.

Finally the hunter's day arrived. At the edge of an open field he spotted a magnificent buck with a huge rack. It was the most exciting moment of his life. None of his friends had ever gotten a deer as fine as this.

Slowly he drew his rifle up to his shoulder, aimed carefully, and squeezed the trigger. A moment later, the buck fell to the ground.

The hunter let out a pathetic imitation of a Tarzan yell and ran across the field. The deer was huge. And he had been right—it was an eight-point buck. If only his friends had gone hunting with him. Fortunately, he had brought a camera along. He propped up the deer's head, and rested his rifle in its antlers. Then he stepped back to mount the camera on a tree stump and set the timer.

As the timer buzzed, the hunter hurried over and crouched down beside the deer. A moment later, the camera went off, taking a series of beautiful shots of the buck coming to, standing up and bounding into the forest with the hunter's rifle still in its antlers.

The Hunter's Nightmare

A deer hunter had spent all day tramping the woods and fields of northern Michigan but did see a single deer. In the late afternoon, he decided enough was enough.

As he was driving home, a deer leapt in front of the car. The hunter slammed on the brakes, but he struck the deer anyway. The impact threw the deer's body into a gully along the side of the road.

The hunter got out of his car to inspect the damage. Miraculously, his front end was intact. Then the hunter had an idea. He could still go home with a kill—he just wouldn't say how he had killed the deer. He dragged the deer out of the gully and stuffed it into the back seat of his car.

A few miles down the road, the deer came to. As the terrified animal thrashed around inside the car, the panicked hunter grabbed a tire iron and swung wildly at the deer. He missed, and hit his dog in the head. The dog snarled and sank his teeth into his owner's arm. Somehow the man had managed to pull over to the side of the road. He ran from the car, pursued by his angry dog, and took refuge in a phone booth. He dialed 911.

"There's a deer in the back seat of my car kicking out all the windows!" he shouted into the phone.

"Sir," the 911 operator said, "I'm not sure how we can remedy this situation."

"Just send some cops! If they shoot the deer, I'll split the meat with them."

Don't Drink the Water

Two 10-year-old boys who lived in rural Montana went on a hike in the woods near their homes. Around noon they stopped by a stream to eat lunch. When they finished, both boys knelt beside the stream, cupped their hands, and drank some of the icy cold water.

"Snakes!" one of the boys yelled.

There, on the edge of the stream, was a nest teaming with baby snakes. The boys scrambled up the bank and ran for home.

A few months later, long after they had forgotten about the snake nest, one of the boys became very sick. He had severe stomach cramps. He was always hungry, yet he kept losing weight. His concerned parents took him to a pediatrician who sent him to the local hospital for a series of tests.

After studying an x-ray, a surgeon told the boy's parents that he was going to operate immediately.

"I'll explain everything after surgery," he said. "I can't waste any time."

In the operating room, the surgeon warned the rest of his surgical team.

"I don't want to frighten you, but be prepared for something out of the ordinary," he said.

Without any further explanation he cut open the boy's abdomen and removed a live, full-grown water snake.

The Watch Dog

This legend is at least 1,000 years old and is told in virtually every part of Europe. In Wales, the heroic dog's name is Gellert. In France, the dog's name is Guinefort. There is evidence that for many years French peasants prayed to Saint Guinefort to protect their children from harm.

After the death of his wife, a fur trapper took his infant and his large sled dog and moved to a cabin high in the Canadian Rockies, miles from any town or homestead. While the man set and checked his traps, the dog guarded the baby.

One winter's day while the hunter was out on his rounds, a blizzard struck. It took him hours to slog his way through the snow drifts back to his cabin. When he arrived, he found the door ajar. Cocking his rifle, he rushed into the house. To his horror, he saw the baby's crib overturned and no sign of the child. From behind the bed, crept the trapper's dog, its fur matted with blood.

With a cry of anger and despair, the trapper shot his dog dead. Then the trapper heard the sound of his baby crying. He looked behind the bed and saw his son, safe and unharmed, lying on the floor. And sprawled beside the child was the body of a huge timber wolf, dead where the trapper's dog had killed it.

The Groaning Cactus

Southern California is basically desert, and it takes a lot of water—all of it imported from somewhere else—to keep the area's lawns and gardens green. Some residents would rather work with southern California's environment, so they build rock gardens around their homes and plant cactus and other native plants that require little water.

A woman new to the area decided that she would take the rock-garden-and-cactus approach to landscaping her new home. But when she visited local nurseries she found that a mature cactus cost thousands of dollars. She still wanted a cactus, but she didn't want to spend that kind of money for one. So she came up with an alternative.

She enlisted the help of a guy on her street and together they drove her 4x4 out to the desert. In time, they found the perfect cactus, about five-feet tall. They dug it up, balled the roots, placed it carefully in the 4x4 and headed home where they planted it in the garden that night.

The next morning, as the woman was sipping coffee on her patio and admiring her garden, she heard a faint moaning sound that seemed to be coming from the cactus. As she got closer, she noticed that the needles were quivering. It unnerved her, but she convinced herself it was just the breeze and went back into the house.

The next day the eerie sounds from the garden were considerably louder, and the cactus seemed to be heaving, as if it were trying to break loose from the ground. But once again, the woman convinced herself it was all in her imagination.

On the third day, high-pitched shrieks were emanating from the cactus and the sides of the plant were throbbing. Frightened, almost hysterical, the woman dialed 911.

"The cactus in my yard is alive!" she shrieked. "It's moving and making screaming sounds!"

"Stay indoors, ma'am," the 911 operator said. "I'll get a pest control emergency team over there in a couple of minutes."

The woman had scarcely hung up the phone when a large white van from the Department of Animal Services pulled into her driveway. Four men in heavy protective gear stepped out of the van and hurried into the back yard. Ignoring the advice of the 911 operator, the woman ran outside to meet them. One held a chain saw; the others carried canisters that resembled fire extinguishers.

"It's that one!" she said. "The one having convulsions!"

"Step back!" the crew shouted at her. "Get back in the house!"

Then, just as the man was about to fire up the chain saw, a loud, ugly ripping sound filled the yard and hundreds of poisonous tarantulas spilled out of the ruptured cactus.

The Mysterious Break-In

A family returned home one afternoon to find a huge hole in their roof and their dog dead in the living room, surrounded by a huge puddle of urine. Nothing was missing and no other damage had been done to the house.

The bewildered family called the police who were just as puzzled when they inspected the scene. At the family's request, the police department conducted an investigation.

Several weeks later the detective in charge of the investigation dropped by with the report.

"The key to solving this case was the urine," the detective said. "Our guys in forensics analyzed the samples and found that it represented the urine of a couple hundred individuals—men, women, and children."

"That makes no sense," the mother of the family said. "Why would 200 people come into our house to do nothing but urinate, kill the dog, and make a hole in the roof?"

"No one came into your house," the detective said. "And I'll explain why in a minute, but first, do you get a lot of plane traffic around here?"

"Oh yeah," the father said. "Planes are flying over the house everyday. This must be one of the main approaches to LaGuardia."

"We thought so. You see, a plane was coming in for a landing at LaGuardia. It jettisoned the urine from its toilets. As the fluid dropped through the atmosphere, it froze. The block of frozen urine crashed through your roof, and struck and killed your dog. By the time you returned home, the ice had melted and formed the huge puddle of urine you found on your living room floor."

The Guest and the Dog

A woman who had just moved with her family to Belair was delighted when she received an invitation to tea at the home of one of the wealthiest and most socially prominent ladies in the community.

As the guest walked up to the front door, she encountered a large, shaggy, filthy dog. The pooch followed the woman up the front steps and sat down beside her. The hostess opened the door, but her smile of welcome faded when she saw that her guest had come to the house with a very dirty mutt. Nonetheless, she threw wide the front door. The newcomer stepped into the foyer, and the dog followed.

While the two women chatted and tried to ignore the dog, the animal ate finger sandwiches and cookies from the serving dishes, put its muddy paws on the furniture, and chased the cat through the house.

Finally the guest was so uncomfortable that she made her excuses and got up to leave.

"Don't forget to take your dog," said the hostess, who had exercised heroic self-restraint throughout the visit.

The guest stared at the woman.

"My dog!" the guest said. "I thought it was yours!"

The Flying Cow

A man had stopped for lunch at a roadside diner in rural Nebraska. After his meal he went out to the parking lot and found the hood of his car crushed, with the body of a dead heifer sprawled across it. Soon the entire diner had emptied out as everyone speculated how such a thing could have happened.

Meanwhile the man went back inside to call his insurance company.

"I want to report an accident," said the man.

"Please describe the nature of the accident," said the insurance company's customer service representative.

"The front of my car was crushed by a cow."

"I see. You hit a car while you were driving."

"No," the man said. "The car was parked in a lot outside a diner. I was not even in the car at the time of the accident."

"Sir, how did the cow get onto the hood of your car?"

"I don't know," the man said. "It must have dropped onto the car."

"You're saying a flying cow landed in your car?"

"Not flying," the man said. "Cows can't fly. Something must have flung it in the air."

"So someone flung a cow onto the hood of your car."

"Yes," the man said. "That must be it."

The insurance company rep sighed.

"Sir, we'll have to investigate this accident and get back to you," he said.

Several days later the man received a phone call at his home from the same customer service rep.

"Sir, it appears that your car was indeed struck by a flying cow. The same day you called we received a claim from a trucking company. One of their drivers hit a cow near the diner where you were eating. The trucker saw the cow fly through the air, but he didn't know where it landed. We'll be sending out a check to you today."

The Flying Kitten

A young couple found a kitten in their backyard and decided to adopt it. One day the little thing escaped out the back door and raced up a tree. Coaxing, food, toys, catnip—nothing would lure the kitten down.

"I have a solution," the husband said. He went into the garage and came out with a long rope. He threw the rope over the branch the kitten clung to and began to pull. The branch bent and the kitten was nearly within the wife's reach when the rope snapped. The branch shot forward like a catapult and the kitten was hurled through the air. The heartbroken couple looked everyone for their pet, but they never found it.

A few weeks later the wife was shopping in the supermarket. At the check-out counter she met one of her neighbors from two blocks away. The neighbor was unloading cans of cat food from her shopping cart.

I didn't know you had a cat," the woman said.

"We didn't until recently," the neighbor said. "About four weeks ago Ralph and I were sitting in the yard when out of no where this kitten flew over our backyard fence and landed safe and sound in Ralph's lap."

The Leashed Dog

It was a 12-year-old boy's job to take the family dog for a walk every day after he got home from school. He liked the dog, and he didn't mind taking it for a walk, but one day a friend stopped by and asked him to go swimming in his family's new pool.

"I've got to walk the dog first," he told his friend.

"No you don't," the other kid said. "Just tie the dog somewhere outside. It can do its business and you can go swimming."

This seemed like a good idea. So the boy walked his dog out to the garage, and tied to the leash to the garage door handle.

An hour later the boy's mother was returning home from an errand. As she turned onto her street, she hit the remote for her garage door. When she pulled into the driveway, she saw the family dog hanging by the neck from the garage door. It was dead.

Variant: In another version of this story, the boy is traveling with his family in a camper. During a lunch break, the boy ties the dog to the rear bumper of the camper, and forgets about the animal. When the family drives away, the dog is dragged to death.

The Unusual Flower Arrangements

A woman had just bought a beautiful house in Los Angles and decided to throw a lavish house-warming party. She found a caterer and hired bartenders and several servers. All she needed was a distinctive decorative element that would make her party memorable.

She went to a fashionable florist and ordered a dozen flower arrangements in large clear glass bowls. Then she went to a pet store and bought several dozen goldfish.

On the morning of her party, the florist delivered the beautiful flower arrangements in large clear glass bowls. While the caterer and the servers and bartenders did the preparation work for the party, the hostess took her gold fish and placed six in each of the flower arrangements. The golden-colored fish looked lovely as they darted among the dark green stems of the flowers.

Soon the guests arrived and each one commented on the hostess' decorative flare. But as the party progressed, the guests become more and more silent, and the hostess found that they were congregating in small groups around each of the flower arrangements. The hostess sidled her way up to one of the little groups. Everyone was staring with glum expressions at the flower arrangement where the gold fish were all floating belly up in the bowl.

"That pet store sold me diseased gold fish," the hostess cried.

"Whether the fish were sick or not," one of her guests said, "they couldn't survive long in those bowls. The flowers sucked all the oxygen out of the water."

The Parakeet and the Splint

A man arrived at a veterinarian's office one morning with his parakeet. The bird had fallen off its swing and broken its leg. The vet placed a tiny wooden splint on the bird's leg, charged the man $35, and sent him home.

Before man and bird arrived home, the parakeet scratched and pecked at the splint until it broke. Back the man went to the vet who put on a new splint and charged the man another $35.

Five times this episode was repeated, and each time the vet charged the man the full $35 fee. So a day or two later, when the parakeet had broken yet another splint, the man felt that he could replace the splint himself.

The only piece of wood he had around the house that was comparable in size to the vet's splint was a wooden match. So the bird's owner bound the bird's leg to the match and returned the bird to its cage. Then he went outside to do some gardening.

The parakeet hopped around its cage scratching and pecking at the splint as usual, but it had the misfortune to drag the match stick against the rough surface of the cage liner. The match ignited, the bird's feathers caught fire, and an hour later when the man came back into the house he found the charred body of the parakeet lying on the floor of the cage.

"Don't Let the Cat Out"

A couple in Seattle was selling their house. They had a beautiful pure-bred Persian cat which they never allowed to go outside. Whenever the couple had to leave the house, they posted a note on the door for the real estate agents: "Please don't let the cat out."

One Saturday morning the husband and wife had a lot of errands to run. They knew at least one real estate agent would be showing their house to prospective buyers that day, so they posted the "Don't let the cat out" note on the front door.

When the couple returned in the afternoon, they found their beautiful Persian in the living room being mounted by a ragged tomcat.

They chased the stray out of the house, and then found this note from the realtor.

"Another agent must have let your cat out by mistake. I found him sitting by the front door, so I let him in."

Three months later, the beautiful Persian cat gave birth to a litter of mongrel kittens.

The Cat Toys

Only a few weeks after a young couple got married, the wife came home with a kitten.

"I don't like cats," the husband said.

"But this one's so sweet," the wife answered. "And I promise never, ever to ask you to clean the litter box."

And so the husband gave in. After a couple of days, he found that he actually liked the kitten. It was a playful little thing. It especially liked to bat balls of yarn with its tiny paws.

The couple and the kitten had been living happily together for three weeks. One morning while the husband was in the shower the wife came into the bathroom.

"The garbage disposal has shut down again," she said. "Come out and reset it."

"I'm taking a shower," the husband told her. "You know where the reset button is."

"But that thing scares me. Please. You're good at these things."

The husband cursed under his breath, and to make a point

walked dripping and naked to the kitchen. He squatted down beneath the kitchen sink and fumbled for the garbage disposal reset button. He never saw the kitten come bounding into the kitchen. But the kitten saw him. Or rather, it saw two balls swaying about a foot off the floor.

The kitten scampered over to the sink, leapt up and sank its needle-like claws into the man's scrotum sack.

With a blood-curdling scream, the husband jumped up, slammed his skull against the underside of the stainless steel sink, and knocked himself out.

The wife rushed into the kitchen to find her husband, wet, naked and unconscious on the kitchen floor and her kitten mewing pitifully, its nasty little claws still caught in the man's scrotum.

When the husband came to, he was strapped to a gurney. All around him were paramedics and cops snorting and trying, unsuccessfully, to suppress their laughter.

"I want a divorce," he said to his wife who was standing at the foot of the gurney, holding the kitten and not saying a word.

JOHN WAYNE WAS A DRAFT DODGER AND OTHER CELEBRITY LEGENDS

John Wayne Was A Draft Dodger and Other Celebrity Legends

The Heckler

In 1970 Grand Funk Railroad was playing an arena in Los Angeles. In the middle of Mark Farner's featured guitar solo, someone in the front of the crowd shouted, "You suck!" and started to boo loudly. Farner kept his cool, and continued to play, but the heckler didn't stop. After a few minutes the booing and the insults were getting to Farner. He put down his guitar, motioned for the band to stop, and walked to the edge of the stage.

"You think you can do better, buddy?"

"Yeah," the heckler said. "I know I can."

"Fine. Get your ass up here and show us how good you are."

The heckler jumped up onto the stage, picked up the guitar, and played B.B. King's classic "Three O'Clock Blues."

The crowd went nuts, and even Farner was impressed. He took the stranger aside and asked him to wait for the band backstage.

After the show, Farner found the mystery guitarist. "You're great. You could make a career for yourself in this business. What's your name, man?"

"I'm Eric Clapton," the heckler said.

The Good Samaritan

Tales of mysterious strangers who come out of nowhere to help in a desperate situation date back at least as far as the Robin Hood legends of Medieval England. They are an especially popular facet of the folklore of the American West.

A traveler got a flat tire on a desolate stretch of road west of Butte, Montana. He did not have a spare tire. He did not have a cell phone and he had no idea how far it was to the next town or gas station.

Hour after hour slipped by, and not single car came along. The traveler was getting pretty nervous and wondered what he should do. Then he heard the rumble of a motorcycle far off in the distance. A few minutes later, a biker, wearing black leather and a shiny black and red helmet, was inspecting the flat tire.

"I can go to the next town and buy you a new tire. It will take me about an hour to get back," he said.

Before the traveler could give the stranger money for the new tire, the biker roared away.

An hour later the biker returned with a brand new tire, and helped the traveler change the flat.

"I'm awfully grateful," the traveler said. "Now, what did that tire cost you?"

"Don't worry about it," the biker said. "I'm glad I could help."

"By the way," the traveler said. "You look familiar. What's your name?"

The biker picked up his shiny helmet.

"I'm Evel Knievel," he said.

Suicide on the Yellow Brick Road

A new employee at a video store was about to play "The Wizard of Oz" on the store TV when his fellow clerks stopped him.

"You don't want to play that movie," the store manager said. "It's got a really disturbing scene."

"You mean the flying monkeys?" the rookie said. "Everybody's use to them by now."

"No," the manager said. "I mean the suicide."

The new guy was stunned. "There's no suicide in The Wizard of Oz," he said.

"Come into my office," the manager said. "I'll prove it to you."

Inside his office, behind closed doors, the manager popped the video into his VCR and hit the fast forward button. He stopped at the scene of Dorothy, the Scarecrow, the Tin Man, and the Cowardly Lion about to set off together down the Yellow Brick Road.

"Look off to the edge of the screen," the store manager said. "There's a man by all those trees."

The rookie looked. A man, not in costume, stood beneath a tree.

From the limb above his head hung a noose. The man climbed onto a wooden chair, but loses his footing. He tried again, got his balance on top of the chair, slipped the noose around his neck and tightened it. After a moment, the man kicked the chair out from under himself.

As Dorothy and her friends skip down the road to see the Wizard, the body of the hanged man swings slowly at the edge of the frame.

The Evil Twin

An Austrian couple were visiting relatives in a remote mountain village when the woman began to go into labor. The nearest doctor was in a town five miles away. While their relatives did what they could to assist the new mother, the husband hurried off to get the doctor.

A few hours later, the husband and the doctor arrived at the house to find that the woman had given birth to twin boys. They were very small, of extremely low birth weight, and they were blue. The doctor sat down beside the mother .

"Frau Hitler, the babies need oxygen, but I only have enough in my medical bag to save one of the children. I must ask you to choose," he said.

The new mother wept and kissed her two babies. Then she

handed over one of the tiny infants.

"Here, doctor," she said. "Save my little Adolph."

The Lucky Landscaper

This story of the celebrity landscaper dates back to the 1940s.

A man had just moved to Beverly Hills and was looking for a good landscaper. One day, as he was driving home, he saw a black man tending a beautifully manicured lawn. The man pulled his car over to the curb and got out.

"Excuse me, " he said as he walked across the lawn, "do you take care of this yard regularly?"

"Every week," said the man with the lawn mower.

"I just moved into the neighborhood and I need a landscaper. So I wanted to ask you Mr...."

"Murphy."

"Mr. Murphy."

"You can call me Eddie."

"Okay, Eddie it is then. So Eddie, how often do you work on this yard?

"Well, the lady of the house is happiest when I do a little work every day."

"And what does she pay you?"

"Nothing. She just lets me sleep with her every night."

Variants: The earliest version on record featured Bing Crosby. In later years the lucky landscaper was Bill Cosby or Flip Wilson.

The Bell Hop at the Plaza

Rev. Jesse Jackson was standing in front of the Plaza Hotel when a cab pulled up. Out stepped a white woman who looked at Jackson and smiled.

"The driver will open the trunk for you. Just leave my bags in the lobby, please," she said.

Without saying a word, Jackson lifted the woman's suitcases out of the trunk of the cab and carried them into the hotel. When he returned to the curb, the woman was waiting for him.

"Thank you," she said. "You're very efficient." Then she handed him three dollars.

"I was happy to help ma'am," Jackson said.

Then, a limousine pulled up and the white driver stepped out to hold the door for the Jackson. As the limo pulled away, Jackson rolled down his window and gave the stunned woman a little wave.

Elvis' Farewell

East of Memphis was a farm owned by the McCoy family. The husband and wife knew Elvis Presley from the time he was a boy. When Elvis was just starting out in the music business in Memphis, the McCoys would have him out to the farm for Sunday dinner. The King never forgot the family's kindness. Even after he became a superstar, he stayed in touch with the McCoy's. When Elvis moved to Graceland, he often drove out to see his old friends. Several times when money was tight, Elvis helped the elderly couple.

One August day, Mr. McCoy was out in the field replacing some rotten fencing. He looked up and saw Elvis walking toward him. It seemed as if Elvis were wrapped in a blue mist, but at the time Mr. McCoy was so glad to see his old friend that he didn't think much of the phenomenon.

"Son, what are you doing out here in the fields in your city shoes? And where's your car?" he asked.

"I just stopped to say good-bye," Elvis said.

"You going back to Las Vegas?"

But before Elvis could answer, Mr. McCoy heard his wife calling him, and she sounded upset. He turned toward the sound of her voice, and when he turned back to ask Elvis to come with him into the house, the King was gone.

By that time, Mrs. McCoy was beside her husband. She was weeping.

"Oh Henry! It's the saddest thing. The man on the radio just said that nice boy, Elvis Presley, was found dead this morning."

Short Takes

• John Wayne dodged the draft during World War II.

• To expand her Living empire, Martha Stewart had herself cloned by a geneticist at Columbia University.

• During a program on how to cook duck, Julia Child dropped one of the birds on the floor. Without batting an eye, she picked up, dusted it off, and placed it back in the roasting pan.

"Never let a little thing like that upset you," she said. "After all, you're alone in the kitchen."

• An episode of "Leave It to Beaver" made history when it showed the first toilet ever to appear on American television.

• The pilot for Gilligan's Island revealed Gilligan's first name was Willy.

• The producers of Sesame Street have decided to make Bert and Ernie a gay couple.

• The creators of Star Trek added the character, Ensign Chekhov, after an editorial in Pravda lambasted the show for failing to have a Russian aboard the U.S.S. Enterprise.

• Raquel Welch came on "The Johnny Carson Show" with a beautiful Persian cat.

"Would you like to pet my pussy?" she asked as she took her seat next to Johnny's desk.

"Sure, if you get that damn cat out of the way," he said.

• In the original 1940s radio program, "The Green Hornet," Kato's character was Japanese. After the Japanese attack on Pearl Harbor, Kato's nationality was changed to Filipino.

• At the end of one of his broadcasts, Uncle Don, the host of a popular children's radio program in the 1930s, failed to notice that he was still on the air.

"There. That ought to hold the little bastards," he said.

• During the course of an interview, pop superstar Mariah Carey expressed her compassion for famine victims.

"I see those poor starving kids all over the world and I just cry. I'd love to be that thin, but not with all those flies and stuff."

• Ronald Reagan was originally cast to play Rick in Casablanca.

• Humphrey Bogart and Ed Sullivan were brothers.

• Humphrey Bogart developed his trademark lisp after his father hit him across the mouth when he was 10 years old.

• Humphrey Bogart developed his trademark lisp in the Navy after an inmate trying to escape from the brig hit him across the mouth with his handcuffs.

• Humphrey Bogart developed his trademark lisp in the Navy after a piece of shrapnel from an attacking Japanese submarine hit him across the mouth.

• During her "Larry King Live" interview, Monica Lewinsky said, "I've learned not to put things in my mouth that are bad for me."

• Star of All My Children, Susan Lucci, is the daughter of Phyllis Diller.

• Outrageous MTV comedian Tom Green had his show canceled after he attended a bar mitzvah dressed as Adolph Hitler.

• Phil Collins wrote "In the Air Tonight" about his brother's drowning. The first time Collins performed the song in concert, he sent free front row tickets to a man who had witnessed the drowning and done nothing to help.

• Phil Collins wrote "In the Air Tonight" about his wife's rape. The first time Collins performed the song in concert, he sent free front row tickets to the rapist.

• The will of movie critic Gene Siskel specified that he must be buried with his thumb pointing up.

THE HALL OF TORTURED SOULS AND OTHER HIGH TECH SCARES

THE HALL OF TORTURED SOULS

Users of Excel 95 found something uncanny in their software, something that has been removed from later versions of Excel. If you have Excel 95, you can experience it yourself. Here's how it works.

1. Open a new file.

2. Scroll down to row 95.

3. Click on the row 95 button which will highlight the entire row.

4. Press tab to move to the second column.

5. With your mouse, click on Help, then click on About Microsoft Excel.

6. Press ctrl-alt-shift and click on the Tech Support button simultaneously.

7. A window will appear with the title, The Hall of Tortured Souls. The hall looks like a scene from Doom. Using your mouse, move around the chamber. On the wall you will see endless lists of names scrolling on the walls under the heading "Tortured Souls."

8. Go to the flight of stairs, walk up the stairs, then come back down and position your cursor in front of the blank wall. Type in EXCELKFA.

9. The blank wall will open to reveal a secret passage. Move carefully down the passage, be careful not to go over the edge. At that end of the passage a terrible secret will be revealed to you.

Intel's Revenge

One evening at a bar, two engineers from Intel were bitching about their favorite villain, Bill Gates, president of Microsoft.

"You guys are so predictable," the bartender said as he bought them a round. "Every night, it's the same song and dance about how awful Bill Gates is. But I got news for you boys, a hundred years from now, Bill Gates is going to be a corporate hero, like Carnegie and Rockefeller. Those guys were SOBs, too, but nobody remembers that now. Why don't you two techno-wizards figure out some way to express your feelings for Bill Gates that will last through the ages."

The two engineers looked at each and they knew the bartender was right. They should be able to create some artifact that would be preserved in museums, something that would tell future generations that Bill Gates had not been everybody's hero.

The next day, they got their chance. Their boss assigned them to create a new version of the Pentium microprocessor.

For the next few months, the two engineers were positively giddy around the office. They came to work early and left late. They worked weekends. They were unfailingly cheerful and the prototype of the new microprocessor they were designing was excellent. All the executives were pleased.

The day PCs with the new Pentium chip went on the market, the two engineers had cases of champagne brought in and threw the wildest office party in the history of Intel.

Months passed and the two engineers were still a happy couple of guys. Then one day, a rumor began to spread through the computer industry that there was a secret message engraved on the new Pentium chip.

Executives at Intel tried to ignore the rumor, but the furor in the industry and the press, coupled with the unusual behavior of the two engineers responsible for the redesign of the chip, made them suspicious. At a special closed session of the company's executive board, the members voted unanimously to select Pentium chips at random and have them analyzed.

A few days later the executive board met again in a closed session.

"Ladies and gentlemen," the CEO said, "as you know analysts in our lab selected a random sampling of one dozen of the new Pentium chips. Examination of the chips under a powerful electron microscope detected the same message engraved on each chip. Here is what they found."

The executives turned toward the large monitor mounted on the board room wall. The CEO struck RETURN on the keyboard in front of him and there appeared a magnified image of the latest Pentium chip.

"BILL SUX" was engraved on it.

The Cupholder

A technical support rep at Apple sat down at her desk and picked up her first call of the day.

"This Apple tech support. How can I help you today?" she said.

"Hi!," said a man on the other end of the line. "The cupholder on my new computer is jammed and I can't get it to close."

"Sir, you did say cupholder, correct?"

"That's right. It was working fine until this morning."

"Okay. First let me ask you a few questions. What model to you have?"

"I have a G4."

"Okay. I'm checking the specs on that model and I do not see a cupholder. Did you have your G4 customized by the dealer?"

No. It was my understanding that this was standard equipment. It's built right in."

The customer service rep was silent for a moment.

"Sir, why don't you describe the location of the cupholder and how it operates."

"Well, there's an oblong button beneath it. When I press the button the cupholder comes out of the machine. It worked fine a few minutes ago, but when I put my coffee cup on it, the tray sagged and now it won't retract."

"Sir, that tray you've been using as cupholder, that's your CD-ROM drive."

Get a FREE Honda!

The get-something-for-nothing-just-by-sending-out-e-mail is a newcomer in the field of urban legends.

To become the number one car manufacturer in the world, Honda has launched an unusual campaign to promote its product.

Log on to the Honda webpage (www.Honda.com) and open an account in your name. Automatically the company will credit $1,000 to your account. For each person you email about Honda, Honda will add $200 to your account. Every time a recipient of your email forwards it to someone else, Honda will credit $100 to your account. Thanks to a powerful new BETA program, Honda will be able to track all of these emails accurately.

In a very short time, you could have enough in your account to get a Honda automobile FREE!

Variants: In other versions of this legand, the energetic e-mailers earn free cases of M&Ms, Pepsi, or Miller beer.

This Time Microsoft Has Gone Too Far

Sophisticated hackers have found proof that Bill Gates' evil empire, Microsoft, has become too cocky. It's not some wacky theory linking Gates with the Antichrist or demonstrating the links between Microsoft, the Rosecrucians, the Freemasons and the Illuminati. Instead, the secret is right where everyone can see it for themselves: in MS Word's Thesaurus function.

Here's how it works.

Type in: "I hope Microsoft will rule the world."

"I should say so," the Thesaurus responds.

Another experiment uncovers Microsoft's fascist agenda.

Type in: "Kill all fags."

"Kill by beheading," the Thesaurus responds.

Type in: "All Jews must die."

"All over," the Thesaurus responds.

Type in: "I'd like all dikes dead."

"I'll drink to that," the Thesaurus responds.

If you have MS Word on your computer, try this yourself! It really works.

The Internet Psychic

In Ohio, a 15-year-old high school girl named Jennifer had a crush on the most popular guy in her school, a handsome football star named Danny. But Danny treated her like dirt. So Jennifer vowed that she would get revenge.

One night while she was answering her email, she had an idea. She would mess with Danny's head.

The next day, she paid her school's best hacker $50 to get Danny's email address. Then she gave him another $100 to keep his mouth shut about it.

That night Jennifer sent Danny an e-mail introducing herself as TawnyK. "I have psychic powers," she wrote. "I know all about you." And to prove it, TawnyK/Jennifer supplied details about Danny's classes, friends, even the location of his locker.

Danny was definitely spooked. Night after night TawnyK sent him email about where he lived, his activities during the day, even what he had said. It was freaking Danny out, so he showed the e-mails to his older brother.

"You moron," Danny's brother said. "It's probably somebody at school."

The next day Danny asked around school about TawnyK, but no one had ever heard of her. Nor would anyone admit to giving out Danny's e-mail address.

Meanwhile, TawnyK/Jennifer decided to make things more interesting. She downloaded porn from the web and sent it to Danny saying she wanted him to perform sexual favors for her. She was always afraid that she would go too far, that Danny would just stop signing on, or would change his e-mail address. But every night he waited to hear from TawnyK.

One Saturday night Danny did not log on. He was at a party— a party to which Jennifer had not been invited. She was sulking in her room when she heard "You've got mail!"

Jennifer opened her mailbox and there was email from TawnyK.

"You bitch!" it read. "How dare you use my name and pretend to have my powers. I am the only TawnyK and I am a psychic. Stop playing your stupid schoolgirl games or I'll make you very sorry."

Jennifer flamed TawnyK, and went back to reading the other messages in her mailbox.

Later that night, when Jennifer's mother came into her room to say good-night, she found her daughter face down on the keyboard. Jennifer was dead.

The autopsy revealed that Jennifer's brain had been fried by a powerful electrical shock. Mysteriously, an inspection of the wiring in her parents' house and of Jennifer's computer showed no trace of even a power surge let alone a deadly jolt of electricity.

Extend the Voters Rights Act!

Most Americans do not realize that the Voters Rights Act President Lyndon B. Johnson signed in 1965 was only an act, not a law. That's why in 1982, President Ronald Reagan extended the Voters Rights Act for another 25 years.

What does this mean? It means that in 2007, when the Act expires, African Americans will lose their right to vote.

The only solution is an amendment to the United States Constitution which will guarantee the right to vote to all American adults irrespective of race. Because it takes the approval of 38 states to amend the Constitution, the Congressional Black Caucus has launched a massive e-mail campaign now to get the word out.

E-mail everyone in your address book and urge them to e-mail their representatives in Congress to begin the process of amending the Constitution. It is the only way to ensure that African Americans will not lose their right to vote.

A Call for Help

A Microsoft tech support representative received a call from a woman who was clearly very angry.

"Please tell me the problem, ma'am," the representative said. "I'll see if I can help you."

"It's about time!" the woman said. "I've been waiting for four hours."

"I'm sorry ma'am, I don't understand. Do you mean you've been on hold for four hours?"

"No! Of course not. I've been working in MS Word and I had a formatting problem so I pressed the Help key. That was four hours ago and I'm still waiting! What I want to know is how long it will take you people to get here?"

Just the Fax

A customer called Dell's tech support with a fax modem problem.

"I've been trying to fax a document for two hours now and nothing happens. I thought this model came with an internal fax modem," the customer said.

"Yes it does, sir," the Dell rep said. "Now let's walk through the process step by step and see if we can find the trouble."

Forty minutes later, the tech support rep was still unable to pinpoint the problem.

"Okay sir, tell me very simply how you have been trying to send the fax," the representative said in desperation.

"I've got the document in my hand, I'm holding it in front of the monitor, and I press send but nothing happens!"

High-Tech Short Takes

• The Elf Bowling game (ELFBOWL.EXE) and the Frog-apult game (FROGAPULT.EXE) has a delayed virus attached to them that is activated every year on Christmas Day. It has already wiped out thousands of computer systems, including the databanks of the Royal Bank of Scotland!

• Do you know a child who is ill with cancer? Send an email about him or her to the American Cancer Society. The organization will donate 3 cents toward the treatment of the child for each e-mail request it receives.

• Amy Jones, the mother of 5-year-old Kelsey Brooke Jones, wants you to help her find her missing child. E-mail everyone in your address book. Someone you know may have seen this little girl.

• Every December 25, unlucky computer users find an e-mail entitled Lump of Coal. Once they open it, the message unleashes a powerful virus that destroys their operating system.

• Atheists are targeting the computers of religious people, sending them an email entitled "It takes guts to say the name JESUS." Once the user opens the e-mail, a virus devastates the computer's memory and the software.

• A congressman has introduced a bill which will charge a postage fee for every e-mail computer users send. The congressman submitted the bill in response to complaints from the U.S. Postal Service that it was losing $230 million in revenue every year because of e-mail.

• Every year on the last day of February, the Internet shuts down for 24 hours for housekeeping that eliminates dead e-mail, and inactive ftp, www and gopher sites.

• To express their outrage at AOL's ever rising prices, hackers will format an online riot next May 1 by sending viruses to thousands of AOL subscribers, shutting down chat rooms, and terminating accounts.

• An email entitled "How to Give a Cat a Colonic" may look amusing but it is anything but funny. Once you open the message, a powerful virus is released that erases all the documents and applications on the hard drive. It also destroys Netscape Navigator and Microsoft Internet Explorer.

• Anyone can log on to the list of Coke machines website and get the commands that will make any Coca-Cola vending machine deliver unlimited cans of Coke—FREE!

• A book was published in May 1994 with the e-mail addresses of movie stars and other celebrities.

• Compaq is considering changing the command "press any key" to "press return key" because so many Compaq users call tech support asking where the any key is.

• In an effort to improve his image, Bill Gates will give a $1,000 and a free copy of the latest version of Windows to anyone who sends a Bill-positive e-mail to 1000 people.

THE $250 COOKIE RECIPE AND OTHER CULINARY MISADVENTURES

THE $250-COOKIE RECIPE

A mother and daughter were having lunch in the bistro of the Neiman-Marcus department store in Dallas, Texas. For dessert, they each ordered the Neiman-Marcus Cookie. From the first bite, the women knew they had found cookie nirvana. It was sweet, filled with rich chocolate and finely chopped nuts, and something else that they couldn't quite make out. So the mother called their waitress.

"This is a delicious cookie," the woman said. "We would love to have the recipe."

"I'm sorry," the waitress said. "We aren't permitted to give out the recipe."

"Well, if you can't give me the recipe, could you sell it to me?"

"Let me find out," the waitress said, and she walked away.

A few moments later she returned, beaming.

"Yes, ma'am. My manager says we can sell you the recipe. The price is two fifty."

"Wonderful! Just charge it to my Neiman-Marcus account."

Four weeks later, the woman's Neiman-Marcus bill arrived. When she opened it she was shocked to find an item from the bistro for $250. She called the store's billing department immediately.

"There's been a typographical error," the woman told the customer service representative. "I purchased the Neiman-Marcus Cookie recipe for two dollars and fifty cents and it was recorded on my bill as two hundred and fifty dollars."

"I'm sorry, ma'am," the customer service representative said. "But the correct price for the cookie recipe is two hundred and fifty dollars. The recipe is unique to Neiman-Marcus and to keep it out of general circulation, the store charges a very high premium to anyone who wants a copy."

"Well, then I'll return it!" the woman said. "I'm not paying $250 for a cookie recipe!"

"Unfortunately, ma'am, the recipe is not a returnable item," the customer service representative said. "Consider it from the store's point of view. You've had the recipe for four weeks, by now you could have copied it and distributed it to everyone you know. I'm afraid I can't help you."

The woman was livid. She felt that she had been purposely misled by the store. But something the customer service representative said gave her an idea. She sat down at her computer and typed up the recipe. Then she e-mailed it to everyone she knew and encouraged them to do the same. Here is the recipe:

2 cups butter

2 cups regular sugar

2 cups brown sugar

4 cups flour

5 cups blended oatmeal*

3 cups chopped walnuts

4 large eggs

2 tsp. vanilla

1 tsp. salt

2 tsp. baking soda

1 8oz. Hershey bar, grated

24oz chocolate chips

* measure oatmeal, then blend in blender until a fine powder

Cream butter and both sugars together.

Blend in eggs and vanilla.

Add flour, oatmeal, salt, and baking soda. Mix well.

Stir in grated chocolate, chocolate chips, and chopped nuts.

Roll batter into small balls and place two inches apart on a cookie sheet.

Bake at 375 for 10 minutes.

Makes approximately 112 cookies.

Straight from the Can

The mother of a high-school girl was a meticulous lady who insisted that all beverages be drunk from a proper glass, not straight from a bottle or can.

"If you are away from home and there is no glass available, make sure you wash off the top of the can before you drink from it," the woman warned her daughter. "There's no telling what nastiness gets on those cans."

The teenage girl, of course, found her mother's rules boring and pointless. Everyday she bought a can of soda from a corner deli and drank it as she walked home from school without cleaning the top of the can.

One afternoon, the girl followed her usual routine. She stopped at the deli and bought a can of soda. The first sip tasted strange, but she did not give it a second thought.

A few blocks later, she began to feel sick, but she kept drinking the soda.

"The caffeine will help settle my stomach," she thought. Before she reached the next street she had severe stomach cramps. "I'll gulp it down then I'll burp and the cramps will go away," the girl thought.

She took a long slug of the soda, emptying the can. A few moments later she staggered and fell face down on the sidewalk.

A cop who was driving down the street saw the girl fall. He called for an ambulance. The ambulance crew strapped the girl to the gurney. "Hand me her backpack so we can find out who she is," one of the paramedics said to the cop. "And give me that soda can, too, just in case."

The girl's mother was terribly upset when she received the call from the emergency room saying her daughter was there and unconscious. She drove to the hospital as quickly as she could. When she arrived, the medical team that had treated her daughter was waiting for her.

"I'm very sorry," the emergency room doctor said. "We did everything we could, but the toxin you daughter ingested works very fast."

"What do you mean toxin?" the poor woman cried. "Was she poisoned?"

"When the police and the paramedics found your daughter, she had an empty soft drink can in her hand," the doctor said. "Our lab tested it and found rat urine on the top of the can. It's a deadly, fast-acting toxin. Your daughter was dead by the time the ambulance got here."

The Package of Cookies

A New York woman was early for her train home, so she stepped into a coffee shop, ordered a cappuccino, and bought a small package of cookies.

All the tables in the café were occupied, but there was a seat at a small table opposite a well-dressed man who was reading a newspaper.

"There are no other seats," the woman said. "Do you mind if I join you?"

"Not at all," the man said. Then he went back to reading his newspaper. He paid no attention to the woman until she opened her package of cookies. He folded his newspaper and set on the table beside his coffee.

The woman took a cookie from the package. Without saying a word, the man took a cookie from the package.

The woman was utterly speechless. She had never seen such effrontery.

She glared at the man as she took a second cookie from the package. He returned her stare and took a cookie, too.

Finally, when there was only one cookie left, the man picked it up, broke it in two and offered half to the woman.
"Please. I insist," he said.

The woman lost her self control.
"You insist! You help yourself to my food and then try to make a gallant gesture! You are the most insufferable oaf I've ever met!"

"I'm insufferable?" the man shouted back. "Who opened my package of cookies and began to eat them?"

"No one!" the woman cried. "Look! Your package of cookies is still sitting there unopened on your briefcase!"

The Lab Report

Two biologists at UCLA went to dinner one night at a hole-in-the-wall restaurant in Los Angeles' Chinatown. One was a vegetarian, and the other a determined carnivore.

Half way through their meal, the carnivore brought up his favorite topic.

"How you can you not eat meat? You have no idea what you're missing. This is the best stir-fried beef I've ever had. The meat is so tender and delectable."

"You want to eat meat," the vegetarian said. "Fine. But I think you're insane ordering meat in a place like this. Stick with the vegetables and rice. At least then you know what you're eating."

"I do know what I'm eating," the carnivore replied. "I've been eating meat all my life. And this is beef."

"Since you're so certain, you wouldn't mind placing a little bet?"

"No, of course not. What did you have in mind?"

"Pick a bone off your plate and let me analyze it back at the lab."

"Okay by me," the carnivore said. "But I get to watch the whole procedure. You might switch bones on me."

After dinner, the carnivore pulled a bone off his plate, wrapped it in a paper napkin, and handed it to his colleague.

Back at the lab, the vegetarian conducted a series of tests under the watchful eye of his meat-eating friend.

"Well, you've submitted it to half-a-dozen tests. Don't you trust your results?" the carnivore said.

"After half-a-dozen tests, yes, I do trust them," the vegetarian said. "I can say with complete confidence that tonight you dined on rat."

Discount Tuna

A woman in Toronto was shopping at her favorite warehouse supermarket when she saw a special sale: a case of brand-name tuna for only $20. She was delighted, and congratulated herself for spending the money on a warehouse membership so she could take advantage of such great bargains.

Back at home, she took out one of the cans to make herself tuna salad for lunch. She chopped up fresh celery and onion, threw in a handful of fresh parsley and a judicious amount of mayonnaise. Then she poured herself a glass of mineral water, sat down at her kitchen table, and took the first forkful of tuna salad.

The tuna tasted a bit odd to her.

"I probably put in too much celery," she said to herself. She went on eating, but the peculiar taste became more and more pronounced. Suddenly the woman felt a sharp pain in her stomach. She jumped up and barely made it to the kitchen sink before becoming violently ill.

After the vomiting subsided, she rinsed out her mouth and went into the living room to lay down on the couch.

She threw up all afternoon, and stomach pangs kept her awake most of the night. The next morning, however, she felt much better. She dumped the rest of the tuna salad down the garbage disposal and washed out the tuna fish can. As the woman rinsed the can, the label peeled off. But beneath the name-brand label, instead of a bare tin can, the woman saw another label that read "Generic Cat Food—Made from Decomposing Fish Parts."

Short Takes

• Bananas imported from Costa Rica are contaminated with necrotizing fasciitis, a bacteria that devours human flesh.

• The U.S. government forced Kentucky Fried Chicken to change its name to KFC because the meat the fast food giant was serving to its customers was so pumped up with additives it could not truthfully be called chicken.

• Kentucky Fried Chicken (in its pre-KFC days) paid millions of dollars to a customer who found a fried rat in his bucket of chicken.

• Never eat pizza in Scandinavian countries. The ground meat topping is actually dog food.

• The first McDonald's in Scandinavia was sued after garbage collectors found hundreds of empty dog food cans in the restaurant's dumpster.

• McDonald's places a small amount of a narcotic in its food to make it addictive.

• Little Mikey died from eating Pop Rocks and drinking soda.

• The secret ingredient in France's finest and most expensive wines is human blood.

• Because it is made from prunes, Dr. Pepper is a soft drink and a laxative.

• Mountain Dew shrinks testicles and makes men impotent.

• Mountain Dew is an effective spermicide.

• Coca-Cola is an effective spermicide.

• If you leave a human tooth in a glass of Coke overnight it will dissolve by morning.

• Coca-Cola paid millions of dollars to a woman who found a dead mouse in her bottle of Coke.

• When it was first manufactured, Coca-Cola contained cocaine.

• Green M&M's are an aphrodisiac.

• Tropical Fantasy, an inexpensive fruit drink that is sold exclusively in minority neighborhoods, is owned by the Ku Klux Klan and contains a drug that causes sterility.

• Hostess Twinkies aren't baked; they congeal like Jello.

THE HOME-MADE LIE DETECTOR AND OTHER BIZARRE CRIMES

THE HOME-MADE LIE DETECTOR

This urban legend was dramatized in an episode of NYPD Blue.

Chicago police had arrested a suspected drug dealer. Although the suspect wasn't a very bright guy, he was stubborn. The arresting officers were getting nowhere with him. Finally, one of the cops had an idea.

He left the room and returned with a portable copy machine and a blood pressure monitor.

"Okay Willie," the cop said, "if you're telling the truth, you won't mind taking a lie detector test. Right?"

Willy looked worried, but he didn't see how he had much of a choice. He agreed to the test.

The cops wrapped the blood pressure band around Willy's upper arm, pretended to plug it into the copy machine, and began the test.

"We found a kilo of cocaine on you, Willy," the cop said. "Where did you get it?"

"It's not mine," Willy answered. "My brother asked me to hold it for him."

The cop hit the copy button and the machine printed out a sheet of paper bearing the word LIE.

"You were going to sell the coke, weren't you, Willy."

"No. I was just holding it for my brother."

Once again the machine printed out a sheet of paper bearing the word LIE.

Willy panicked.

"Your machine is messed up! I don't do coke! I don't sell coke! I don't know no dealers!"

Now the machine pumped out three sheets of paper, each one bearing the word LIE.

"Alright! I was gonna sell it. But I never was dealing before."

Once again, the machine printed out a sheet of paper bearing the word LIE.

The Shopping Mall Con Artist

Two weeks before Christmas 1999, a woman drove her new BMW to a shopping mall near her home in suburban Maryland. As she walked away from her car, a beautiful, well-dressed young woman wearing a button that read Chanel Sales Representative approached the shopper.

"Good morning!" the young woman said. "I represent Chanel and I want to tell you about an exciting holiday offer. Today only, you can purchase Chanel's new fragrance, Chanel 2000, which usually retails for $75 for only $8. Would you like to sample the perfume?"

The shopper was intrigued. She let the Chanel representative spray her wrist. But when the shopper smelled the perfume, she began to feel woozy and passed out.

When she came to, she was surrounded by paramedics, mall security and other shoppers.

"You'll be all right ma'am," one of the paramedics said. "You inhaled a powerful anesthesia. Thieves presenting themselves as Chanel representatives have been victimizing shoppers for weeks now."

"Thieves!" the woman said. "What do they steal?"

"Ma'am," said one of the security guards, "your wallet is missing from your handbag. How much cash did you have on you?"

"I had $800 plus all my credit cards," the woman answered.

"And there's something else, ma'am," the security guard said. "Your car keys are missing."

"That can't be!" the woman said. "I left my new BMW right there." And she pointed to an empty parking space.

Variants: A man invites female shoppers to be in a pizza commercial, or an anti-drug public announcement or to help with a sick child. When the women follow the man outside the mall, they are robbed, abducted, or murdered, depending on who is telling the story.

The Cat in the Bag

A college girl was driving through the parking lot of a mall in Connecicut with a friend when her car accidentally hit and killed a cat.

"We can't just leave it here," one of the girls said.

"I have a shovel and a big Nordstrom shopping bag in the trunk," the girl driving the car said. "We can put the body in the bag and find some proper place to dispose of it."

She pulled the car into a nearby parking space. The girls scooped the dead cat into the Nordstrom shopping bag, and began walking around the outside of the mall looking for a dumpster.

"This wandering around is a waste of time," the driver said. "Let's just ask that security guard where we can find a dumpster."

"Fine," her friend said. "But leave the bag somewhere. We don't want him to see that we're trying to get rid of a dead cat."

They left the Nordstrom bag by a door to the mall and approached the guard. While they were talking to him, a woman hurried up to the Nordstrom bag, looked around quickly, then took the bag and started running across the parking lot.

The girls saw her and began to laugh.

"Let's follow her," the driver said. "I want to see the look on her face when she discovers what she's stolen."

They trailed the woman across the parking lot and saw her duck behind a large SUV. A moment later they heard screaming. The two girls hurried over to the scene, followed by other shoppers who were in the parking lot. The woman was lying on the ground, out cold.

One of the shoppers who had a cell phone called 911. As the paramedics rolled the woman into the ambulance, she regained consciousness and began to scream.

"The bag! The bag!"

The kind shopper who called for help picked up the Nordstrom bag and slipped it inside the ambulance just before the door closed.

"The poor dear," the shopper said to the two college girls. "I wonder what was in that bag."

Six Inches of Steel

This urban legend is probably the basis for a famous scene from the movie, "Crocodile Dundee."

A college student got a summer job playing a knight at a Renaissance festival in New Jersey. Every morning he got up, put on his costume of chain mail and strapped a 36-inch sword around his waist. Then, so he wouldn't look too weird on mass transit, he pulled on a long duster that reached to his ankles and covered his costume.

After a long day of jousting and rescuing damsels at the festival, the student caught a late train to New York. By the time he got on a subway for the final leg of his journey back to his apartment, it was nearly 1 a.m. and he was the only passenger is his subway car.

Suddenly, between stations, a door at the end of the car crashed open. A hulking mugger with a knife in his hand ran up to the student, pulled him to his feet and held the knife in front of his face.

"I've got six inches of steel that says you're going to give me your wallet," the mugger said.

The student reached inside his coat and pulled out his sword. "I'll see your six inches," he said, "and raise you thirty."

The Missing Gnomes

A lady in Arkansas decorated her garden with seven cement figurines of gnomes. One morning when she went outside to get the paper she found that all seven gnomes were gone.

The woman called the police who came out to the house and looked around, but they found no clues of who might have stolen the figurines. They advised the woman to go out buy another set of gnomes.

A few days later the woman received a post card from Hawaii. "We decided we needed a change of scene. Hawaii is beautiful. Having a wonderful time. The Gnomes."

At first the woman was angry that the thief who stole her garden ornaments would play this type of prank on her. Then she noticed that the stamp on the card had been canceled at the post office on

Maui. Now she was confused.

Two weeks later the woman answered her doorbell and found her seven gnomes on the front porch, all of them wearing Hawaiian shirts.

The Greedy Robber

A robber walked into a convenience store in Lawrence, Kansas, pulled a gun on the clerk behind the counter and demanded all the money in the cash register.

The clerk handed the thief $71 in bills.

"I've got about another $10 in change," the clerk said.

"This is it? Seventy-one bucks and change?" the robber said. "Where the hell is the rest of the money?"

"My boss took it to the bank half an hour ago," the frightened clerk said.

The robber thought for a minute.

"Okay. Into the store room," he said. He hog-tied the clerk and covered his mouth with duct tape. Then the robber took the clerk's place behind the counter.

The robber planned to stay only an hour or so, but he raked in over $300 in less than 60 minutes and he got greedy.

"Maybe I should work the kid's whole shift," he thought. "Then I could walk out of here with some serious money."

After three hours, more than $1,000 was stuffed into the cash drawer. The robber was thrilled. But there was one thing he hadn't considered: most of the patrons of the convenience store were regulars. When they saw a strange-looking man ringing up their purchases, they got suspicious.

The robber had just broken the $1,500 mark when four cops burst through the door and arrested him. The newspapers described the crime as the longest hold-up in the history of Kansas.

The Bikers and the All-American Boys

Forty big, loud, hairy biker dudes and their women barreled into a grocery store on a country road in Pennsylvania. The owner of the store was frightened as he watched these unruly customers scatter through the aisles and bring armloads of beer, soda, ice, potato chips, white bread, baloney and mustard up to the counter.

While the bikers were still shopping, four clean-cut college students in football jackets came into the grocery store and stood quietly to one side, waiting for the bikers to finish. The presence of these college jocks made the store owner feel a little more at ease. He even managed to smile at his biker customers and make a little small talk. By the time the bikers were finished, they had spent more than $400 in cash.

After the bikers had roared off down the road, the store owner turned to the four all-American boy.

"Boy, am I glad to see them gone," he said.

"So are we!" one of the college boys said. Then they all reached under their jackets and pulled out pistols. "Now hand over the cash!"

The Jogger's Wallet

A Wall Street executive was taking his early morning run on the narrow jogging path around New York's Central Park Reservoir. Suddenly another jogger coming from the opposite direction clipped him, almost knocking him off his feet. The man regained his balance, then checked his pocket for his wallet. It was gone.

He sprinted after the other runner, caught up to him, grabbed him by the shoulder.

"Hand over that wallet!" he demanded in the loudest, nastiest voice he could muster.

The runner looked frightened and gave the man the wallet immediately.

His adrenaline pumping and his ego swelling by the minute, the Wall Street executive ran two miles more than usual, then headed for his apartment on Central Park West. He took the stairs instead of the elevator and ran into his apartment, sweaty, out of breath, but still flushed from the excitement.

From the kitchen his wife called.

"I thought you'd come back sooner. Didn't you notice you forgot to take your wallet?"

The Double Theft

This story originated in England

A woman spent the morning shopping at Harrod's department store. Before she left for home, she stopped in the ladies room. Inside the stall, she set her purse on the floor and made herself comfortable.

A moment later, a hand reached under the partition and snatched the purse. By the time the poor shopper made herself presentable and found a security guard the thief was long gone. At least the store called her a taxi and paid for the fare.

When she returned home, the building superintendent let the woman into her apartment. She had barely begun to make herself a cup of tea when the phone rang.

"Mrs. Waverly? This is Mr. Morison at Harrod's. We've found your purse. Would you like to come down to the store to collect?"

Naturally, the woman was relieved. She borrowed cab fare from a neighbor and returned to the store. But as it happened her purse had not been found at Harrod's. Furthermore, there was no Mr. Morison employed there.

Now the poor lady was upset. She hurried home where she

found her front door wide open, her keys in the lock, her purse on the table and all of her valuables gone.

The Grateful Car Thief

One morning a couple discovered that their car had been stolen from their driveway. They called the police, but the cops offered them little hope that the car would ever be recovered.

"It's probably been stripped and sold for parts by now," said one of the police officers.

But two days later, the car reappeared in the driveway, perfectly intact, with an envelope taped to the dashboard.

"Forgive me for taking your car. It was an emergency. I can't go into the details, but you ought to know that a life was saved. As a token of my appreciation and to compensate you for your trouble, please accept these theater tickets," a note read.

"These are front row seats to the hottest show on Broadway!" the wife said.

That Saturday night, the couple drove into New York City and enjoyed a wonderful evening.

It was after midnight when they finally returned home. The husband unlocked the front door.

"That was great. I wonder how we can get these people to steal our car every week," he said.

But the couple's euphoria disappeared when they stepped inside their house. All their valuables were gone—the computers, televisions, stereo equipment, silver, jewelry, antiques. And scrawled on the mirror over the fireplace was this message.

"Hope you enjoyed the show!"

Wagger

The wife of a paramedic was accustomed to her husband being called to an emergency at all hours, but she never got used to him leaving her in the middle of the night. She was frightened to be in the house alone. So the husband went to the animal rescue shelter and brought home a big friendly mutt. They named the dog Wagger.

The next night, shortly after midnight, the paramedic's pager went off.

"It's another accident on the highway," he said to his wife. "At least now you have Wagger to protect you."

"Protect me!" the wife said. "This big, drooling furball? He's the lousiest guard dog in town. Why didn't you adopt a nice pit bull?"

The paramedic didn't answer. He just kissed his wife and left the house.

A few hours later the woman woke up to the sound of shattering glass. She could hear someone climbing in a window downstairs.

Wagger heard the intruder, too. He stood at the bedroom door, growling. The woman didn't know what to do. She was afraid to go downstairs and she felt helpless waiting in her bedroom.

Before she could make up her mind, she heard someone climbing the stairs. The intruder was coming directly to the woman's room. She watched in horror as the door knob turned and the door swung open. In the darkness she could make out a large dark figure. "Get him, Wagger!" she screamed.

The dog leapt upon the intruder and knocked him to the floor. The woman ran to the phone and called the police.

"Call him off! Call him off!" she could hear the man shouting. Suddenly the intruder stopped shouting and Wagger trotted over and sat down beside his mistress.

When the police arrived, they pronounced the intruder dead. Wagger had ripped open the man's throat.

"Take his mask off," one of the detectives said. As the cop removed the ski mask, the woman began to weep.

"Do you know this man?" the detective asked.

"He's my husband," the woman said.

"Why would your husband break into his own house," the detective said.

"I think he wanted to prove that Wagger is a good guard dog."

The Thief at the Wedding Reception

After dating for three years, a young couple from northern New Jersey got married. At the reception, guests approached the bride and handed her small white envelopes stuffed with cash, all of which she slipped into a large white silk bag.

At the end of the evening, when the bride and groom were in their hotel room, the bride could not find her silk bag. They called the reception hall, their parents, every member of their wedding party, but no one had the bag, nor had any one seen it. Clearly someone had stolen it.

The unhappy bride wept all night long.

The next day, the couple went off on their honeymoon to Aruba. After a few days, the sting of being robbed at their wedding began to diminish. They had a wonderful time together, and when they returned home they were resolved not to think of the theft any more.

A day or two after the newlyweds returned, they received their wedding video in the mail. That night, the husband and wife sat down on the couch together to watch it. About halfway through the footage of the wedding reception, they saw a man approach the head table, slip the white silk wedding purse under his tuxedo jacket, and walk away.

The thief was the bride's father.

The Well-Dressed Thief

A 19-year-old kid lived with his parents and went to college near their house. One night, while his mother and father were out of town, the kid worked until eleven o'clock at the college library. As he walked across the nearly deserted parking lot, someone grabbed him from behind and held a gun to his head.

"Get in your car, drive me to your house and you won't get hurt," the gunman said.

The boy was frightened so he did what he was told. At the house the thief ordered the boy into the cellar, tied him up, gagged him, and then went back upstairs. For the next hour the boy lay helpless cellar listening to the robber ransack the house.

The next morning the boy's parents returned. The thief had stolen computers, televisions, stereo systems, jewelry, silverware and the boy's prize possession—his Versace sweater.

A week later, the police called the family to announce that they had arrested a suspect. They wanted the kid to come down to the station and identify the thief in a line-up.

When the boy looked through the glass, he recognized the thief immediately.

"That's him," he told the detective. "The second on the right."

"That was fast, son," the detective said. "How can you be so sure?"

"Because he's wearing my sweater."

In the Interest of Accuracy ...

Police in Los Angeles arrested a man for armed robbery. A couple hours later the victim came to the police station to see if she could identify the perpetrator.

The suspect was placed in a line-up with five other men.

"The man who robbed me was wearing a ski mask," the victim said. "I never saw his face. But I know I'd recognize his voice."

The detective who was running the line-up ordered each man to say, "Give me the money or I'll kill you."

One of the suspects refused.

"And what makes you better than everybody else," a detective asked him.

"Because that's not what I said!" the suspect answered.

The Burnt Hand

A wealthy widow lived in a fine old house in Philadelphia. One day, a young couple moved into the house next door. They were a friendly young people, especially the husband who offered to do the widow's banking and help her with the heavy housework. The widow appreciated his help and she also enjoyed his company. He was always willing to listen as she talked about her antiques, or her family silver, or the jewelry she had inherited from her great-grand-mother.

One stormy winter evening, the widow built a large fire in her fireplace, but she neglected to remove the poker. An hour later, she finally noticed that the poker was still embedded in the burning logs. The widow was about to take the poker out of the fire when she heard a loud banging on her front door. She unbolted the door, but left the chain in place. On the porch stood a man in a ski mask.

"I've got a gun," the robber said. "Let me in."

The old woman was very frightened.

"No. Please don't come in. I'll give you something valuable."

"It better be good, Granny," the robber said.

"A diamond bracelet. I'll give you an antique diamond bracelet if you go away," she said.

"It's a deal," the robber said. "Hand it over."

He thrust his hand into the narrow opening. Meanwhile the widow hurried to the fireplace, took out the glowing red-hot poker. She thrust into the robber's hand.

The sound of the man's screams mingled with the hiss of his burning flesh. The robber pulled back his hand and ran away. The widow slammed the door shut and bolted it.

The experience had her very upset, so she called her good neighbors next door.

"Mary, could you and Bill come over? The most terrible thing has just happened to me."

"I'm sorry, Mrs. Wentworth, we can't come over now," the widow's neighbor said. "Bill has just come in and his hand is terribly burned."

THE FINAL SPIN CYCLE
AND OTHER
STRANGE DEATHS

THE FINAL SPIN CYCLE

A man in Farmville, Virginia, was not having a good day. Once again he had postponed doing his laundry for weeks, and now he had no clean clothes. Worse, when he went down to the basement he found that his washing machine was broken. He would have to go to the laundromat, the one place he hated above all others.

Frustrated and angry, he filled the trunk and the back seat of his car with his dirty clothes and drove over to the strip mall where the laundromat was located. His only consolation was at least it was the middle of the week and the place would not be crowded. Sure enough, he had the place entirely to himself.

The laundromat had two dozen machines, and the man filled them all. But when he got to the final machine, a washer that held 40 pounds of laundry, he still had 65 pounds of dirty clothes, sheets and towels. No amount of cramming would make the final load fit into the last washing machine. Frustrated, the man climbed up on the machine and began to jump up and down on the 65 pounds of dirty clothes to force them into the 40-pound capacity wash basin. And that's when he did it. One foot kicked the ON button, and the washing machine began to turn.

The spinning laundry formed knots around the man's ankles and sucked him down knee-deep into the machine. He could not free himself. As the agitator went into high gear, the man was thrashed about. He struck his head sharply on a shelf over the washing machine and knocked over an open bottle of bleach. The bleach splashed onto the man's face, blinding him. He was screaming for help now, but no one heard him.

When the washing machine went into its final high-speed spin cycle, the poor man was spun around at 70 miles per hour. He smashed his head on the steel beam behind the washer and was killed instantly.

The Flying Leap

A high school drop-out who worked at a fast-food restaurant dreamed of a career as a professional bungee jumper. If there is such a thing as an Academy of Bungee Jumping, it wasn't located any place near this young man's home, so he decided he would teach himself.

One Saturday morning, he drove around to several hardware stores and bought a couple hundred short elasticized ropes with a hook at either end. Then he went home and in his parents' garage connected all the straps together into two bungee cords, each 85-feet long.

Very early the next morning he put the homemade bungee cords in his car and drove to a railroad trestle that passed above a highway. He secured one end of the cords to the steel beams of the trestle and the other end to his ankles. Then he stood on the end of the bridge, spread out his arms, and with dreams of fame and success as a daredevil, leapt into open space. Moments later, his skull hit the pavement.

As the ambulance crew carted the body away, the two police officers who had been the first to arrive on the scene coiled up the two home-made bungee cords.

"I don't care what you say," one cop said. "You've got to admire the kid's drive and determination. It took time to make two 85-foot bungee cords."

"Yep," the other cop agreed. "Too bad he didn't know the drop from the railroad trestle is only 70 feet."

Launched on the Fourth of July

Three high school seniors from a small town in Oklahoma were looking forward to the Fourth of July. They had pooled their money to buy some expensive fireworks, and they bragged to their friends that they were going to set off a display the whole town could see.

The trouble was finding a suitably prominent launching pad for the fireworks. There was nothing that could be considered a skyscraper in their town, and it being Oklahoma, there was no hill in the vicinity. The only elevated structure that could be seen from every part of town was the fuel storage tank beside the railroad tracks. It seemed awfully mundane for the extravaganza the boys were planning, but it would have to do.

On the evening of the Fourth, the boys climbed to the top of the fuel storage tank with the fireworks in their backpacks. On the ground a couple hundred feet from the tank stood a small crowd of high school kids.

From their perch, the boys could see the fireworks of neighboring towns off in the distance. Their own town did not squander tax dollars on anything so frivolous which pleased the boys—their show would have no local competition.

"Hey! Do you guys smell gas?" one of the boys said as they unpacked the fireworks.

"Of course we smell gas," one of friends said. "We're sitting on top of a gas tank. Now strike a match so we can light the first rocket."

A moment later a huge fireball erupted from the fuel tank.

The three boys got what they wanted. Everybody in town saw their fireworks display.

The Exploding Lighter

This story has circulated in train yards as well as on Navy installations where it has been a cautionary tale about on-the-job safety.

A worker at the railroad yard in Hoboken, New Jersey, always kept his Bic butane lighter in his pants pocket. One icy day in January, the railway worker walked a little too close to a fellow worker who was trying to thaw a switch with a blow torch.

A spark from the blow torch landed on the man's pants and burned through the fabric. When the spark touched the butane lighter it exploded with tremendous force and blew off both of the man's legs.

By the time an ambulance arrived, he had bled to death.

Lightning on the Lake

Three friends went fishing on Caddo Lake in Texas. Two of the three were having a great morning, pulling in one five-pound pike after another. But the third man in the boat, who happened to be a lawyer, wasn't getting so much as a nibble.

Each time one of his friends reeled in another fish, the lawyer would erupt with a string of foul curses in which God and Jesus Christ figured prominently. The other two in the boat were church-going men and they didn't like what they were hearing.

"Settle down," one of them said. "And watch your mouth."

"Show some respect," the second one added.

"The two of you sound like a couple of old ladies," their angry attorney friend answered. "There is no God. And even if there were, why would God give a rat's ass about what one guy in a boat says?"

A few moments later, the sky began to darken and the fishermen heard the deep, low rumble of thunder off in the distance. Suddenly a great bolt of lightning flashed over the water. The other fishermen on the lake headed for shore. The lawyer's friends reeled in their lines and started preparing to get off the lake, too.

"I suppose you think this is the wrath of God," the lawyer said.

"Whether it is or it isn't," one of his friend said, "only idiots stay out on the water in an aluminum boat during an electrical storm. Sit down! We're going in."

The lawyer let loose another barrage of obscenities. "I'll prove there's nothing to worry about," he said. He stood up in the boat, stretched out his arms, turned his face to the dark, angry sky.

"Okay God! Let me have it!" he said.

The next bolt of lightning struck him full in the chest and hurled him out of the boat. His charred corpse hit the water with a large splash and sank beneath the waves.

Bride-and-Seek

It's thought that this story originated in West Palm Beach, Florida, in the mid 1970s.

A boy and girl who had been sweethearts all through high school decided to get married after graduation. The girl came from a wealthy family, and her parents planned an elaborate reception at their mansion in West Palm Beach, Florida.

It was a tremendous party, and toward the end of the evening, the groom, who had had a few drinks, suggested that they play hide and seek. The remaining family and friends were just drunk enough to get into the spirit of the game.

The groom was it and in half an hour he had found everyone except his bride. He and all the guests looked for hours, all through the house, but they couldn't find the girl. The groom was furious that his bride would play such a cruel trick on him on their wedding night. But when the bride still did not turn up the next day, the groom became frightened and called the police.

Weeks went by and still there was no sign of the girl. The groom was almost insane with grief and worry.

One day, months after the wedding, one of the maids at the bride's parents mansions went up to the attic to dust the old furniture the family kept there. In a corner she saw a large trunk, and out of curiosity she opened the lid.

Downstairs the other servants and the family heard horrible screams. The entire household raced upstairs.

"I found her!" the hysterical housemaid shrieked. "I found her!"

Inside the trunk was body of the bride, her mouth still open in a silent scream.

The Ball Pit

A young mother took her son to his favorite fast-food restaurant on his third birthday. After he had eaten his lunch, the mother let her little boy play in the ball pit. A few minutes later he crawled out of the ball pit.

"It hurts, Mommy," he whined and pulled at his pants. But the woman couldn't see anything. By this time, the little boy was crying so she took him home.

Back in the house, she undressed the child and found a red welt on his buttocks. It seemed to the mother that there was some kind of splinter lodged under the skin. She called her pediatrician, but while she made the appointment the little boy began to vomit violently. Then his eyes rolled back into his head. The woman slammed down the phone, picked up her son, and drove immediately to the nearest hospital emergency room.

As soon as they arrived, nurses rushed the little boy into an examining room, but he died a few minutes later. The attending physician examined the welt and found a one-inch piece of hypodermic needle. The doctor sent the needle fragment to the lab for analysis.

An hour later, he found the heartbroken mother.

"The lab report has just came back," he said. "Can you tell me where your son was today."

"He was home with me all morning," the woman answered. "Then I took him out to lunch and let him play in the restaurant's ball pit. That's where complained that something had hurt him."

The doctor took a deep breath.

"I'm sorry to tell you that your son died of a heroin overdose. Someone put a syringe full of heroin into the ball pit, and it just happened to be your little boy who ran into it."

Variant: In another popular version of this story, the little boy encounters a nest of poisonous snakes in the ball pit.

The Water Slide

Four Florida high-school girls, all seniors, decided to cut school and spend the day together at a water park famous for its 300-foot-long water slide.

At 7:30 a.m. on the appointed day, they all piled into a car as if they were going to school, but headed to the amusement park instead. Because they had left so early, they were the first ones there. The parking lot was empty. Since no was around, they changed inside the car into shorts and bikini tops—the perfect clothes for water rides.

While they were waiting, they saw a strange looking man in dark, dirty clothes and greasy hair climb over the fence from inside the park and jump into the parking lot. Thinking he worked there, one of the girls shouted over to him.

"Excuse me! Is the park going to open soon?"

The man looked frightened at first. Then he smiled. "Nine o'clock. They always open the gates at nine o'clock. I've just finished inspecting the rides and everything is ready."

As he walked away, he waved.

"If I were you, I'd go on the water slide first. Have a nice time!" he shouted.

Thirty minutes later, when the gates to the park opened, the four girls were the first in line. After they bought their tickets they rushed to the water slide so they could be the first ones on it.

Four giant slides ran side by side down into a huge swimming pool. From the platform at the top the four girls looked down and shrieked with excitement and anticipation. They took their places at the top of the slides then, at the count of three, all four pushed off together.

A moment later the girls were screaming in pain and the water slide was red with blood. By the time the girls reached the pool at the bottom of the slide, park employees were running over to help them. They lifted them from the water and rushed them to the first aid station but the girls' major arteries had been slashed open. They were already dead.

The park's management closed the ride, shut off the water and conducted a careful inspection. Attached to the bottom and sides of each slide they found a dozen razor blades embedded in chewing gum.

The Hair Fryer

This relatively new urban legend seems to be a spin off of the lady who tried to dry her wet poodle in the microwave.

All through her sophomore year, a high school girl in Miami had had a crush on a boy in her Spanish class. Just before the school year ended, he asked her out on a date.

When the big night arrived, the girl was running seriously late. She had been too long at the mall buying new clothes, and she spent over an hour in the bathtub. Now she had only five minutes to dry her hair and dress.

To save time, the girl ran down to the kitchen, set the micro-wave on "HIGH," and stuck her hair and just the top of her head inside.

Ten minutes later the boyfriend arrived. He rang the bell, but there was no answer. He knocked on the door, but there was still no answer. He called the girl's name, but the house remained silent.

The boy walked around to the back of the house to try the kitchen door. It was open. And lying on the kitchen floor was his date—with the top of her head blown off.

The Lethal Ladies Room

The staff at a Chicago hospital near O'Hare Airport was stumped by three inexplicable deaths. In less than a week, three airline hostesses had been brought to the hospital with the same symptoms: high fever, vomiting, and muscle cramps followed by paralysis and death. Blood showed signs of toxins, but the lab couldn't determine the source of the poison.

The women all worked for different airlines; they had come from different parts of the world before landing at O'Hare. The only thing they had in common was all three had eaten at a restaurant in the airport.

The Department of Health descended on the restaurant and shut it down while they tested the food, the water, the air conditioning ducts, anything that might carry deadly microbes. But they found nothing.

A few days after the restaurant reopened, one of the waitresses showed up at the hospital with the same symptoms as the three women who had died. She said she had had nothing to eat or drink there, she had only stopped by to pick up her paycheck and use the ladies room.

That gave a toxicologist at the hospital an idea. He drove out to the airport to inspect the restaurant's ladies room. All he found was a small spider under one of the toilet seats. It seemed insignificant, but the toxicologist captured the spider and took it back to the hospital.

The spider turned out to be a South American Blush Spider. It is a species that thrives in a cool, damp habitat. And it is extremely venomous.

The toxicologist filed his report with the Chicago Department of Health. They ordered a search of all rest rooms in the airport and of every plane flying in from South America. The other rest rooms in the airport were clean, but Blush Spider nests were found in the rest rooms of four planes.

The Jilted Wife

A wealthy executive lived with his wife on the twentieth floor of a high-rise overlooking Lake Michigan on Chicago's Gold Coast. One evening he returned home from work and announced that he wanted a divorce. He was in love with his 25-year-old secretary and he planned to marry her.

The wife was distracted with grief. She begged her husband not to divorce her. But nothing the poor woman said moved the man. He was determined to have his way. While his soon-to-be-ex-wife wept in the living room, the man packed two suitcases and walked out of the apartment.

"You can live here for the time being. But I'll want this place as part of the divorce settlement," he said on his way out the door.

After the husband slammed the door behind him, the wife burst into a new wave of hysterical weeping. She stumbled out to the terrace, looked at the magnificent view, then climbed over the railing and jumped.

As the woman's husband stepped out of the lobby of the apartment building, he heard a strange sound above him. He looked up and saw his wife's plummeting body—just before it struck and killed him.

The View from the Tower

The first Saturday night after his girlfriend dumped him, a man from Hartford, Connecticut was feeling pretty sorry for himself. He thought he needed a little time alone, a place where he would be far from the noise and demands of the world. From his apartment window, he saw the ideal spot: A 60-foot-high electrical transmission tower.

The man took a cold six pack of beer from his refrigerator, drove to the tower, and climbed up. Near the top he found a small platform where he could sit and think about his life.

After he had finished the fifth beer, the man felt pretty good about himself. But he also felt the urgent need to use the restroom. It didn't seem worth the effort to climb down the tower, so he stood up and unzipped. A beautiful stream arched out over the edge of the platform, and struck one of the high voltage wires.

A charge of electricity, conducted by the urine, traveled up the stream to the source and instantly fried the man. It also knocked out the power for the entire city of Hartford.

A repair crew found the man dead at the base of the tower, his pants unzipped, his private parts charred and still smoking. On the platform they found a single unopened can of beer.

Variant: A related version of this story is set in a city subway station where a drunken man pees off the platform and is electrocuted when his stream of urine hits the third rail.

Fishing for Dummies

A man who lived beside a river in Alabama had invited 20 relatives and friends over for a fish dinner. When he went to the fish market that morning, he discovered it would cost him a fortune to buy enough for so many guests. There had to be a cheaper way to get fresh fish.

On his way back to his car, the man had an idea. At home he got a long pair of cables out of his garage and connected them to the main power source for his house. Then he stood on the riverbank and threw the other end of the cables out into the water. There was a tremendous explosion of sparks as the live cables hit the water, and soon dozens of fresh fish were floating belly up on the surface of the water.

Whooping with joy, the man waded into the river to collect his catch. Sadly, he forgot to reel in the cable. When his dinner guests arrived they found him floating belly up in the water, surrounded by dead fish.

Nothing's Biting Except the Worms

A man out for a walk encountered another man sitting on the bank of a stream, fishing.

"Catch anything?" the passerby asked.

"Nope," the fisherman said.

"What are you using for bait?" the passerby said.

"Just worms," the fisherman answered. "There's a nest of them right here. But instead of the fish biting them the worms keep biting me."

The passerby laughed.

"Nothing's biting except the worms. That's a good one." He continued on his way.

An hour later the man returned from his walk and passed the same stream. The fisherman was still there, but sprawled out face down on the ground, dead. When the passerby rolled over the body, he saw at once what had killed the fisherman. The nest of worms was in fact a nest of baby copperheads.

Pumping

From Thailand comes news of a bizarre new way to get a sexual high. Teenage boys have been inserting the nozzle of a standard bicycle pump up their rectum. The rush of air from the pump is said to cause an intense orgasm.

One boy became addicted to pumping, as it's called. He tried bicycle pumps of different kinds and power in search for the ultimate high. Then one day, on his way home school, he passed a gas station and he had an idea.

Very late that night he slipped out of his house and went to the gas station. Near the back of the lot, hidden in the shadows, he found the compressed air hose. The boy pulled down his jeans, slipped the nozzle up his rectum, set the machine on high and dropped a coin into the slot.

A moment later the entire neighborhood awoke to the sound of a terrible explosion. The first people to arrive at the scene found bits of bloody flesh and a pair of sneakers, but nothing else.

The Backward Jacket

When his mid-life crisis hit, a 45-year-old man went out and bought himself a Harley Davidson motorcycle and a black leather jacket. After his few times out with the bike, the man started wearing his leather jacket backwards. It looked strange, but it was airtight that way and made his ride more comfortable.

One Sunday afternoon, the biker rode up to a lake in the mountains. As he came around a sharp bend in the road, he hit a patch of ice. The motorcycle tipped over and slammed into a tree. The man lay in the road unconscious.

A motorist witnessed the accident and stopped his car to help. He ran over to the biker.

"My God!" the Good Samaritan said, "his head has twisted around!"

So he got a firm grip on the man's head, twisted it back to its "proper" position and broke the cyclist's neck.

The Last One

In the weeks and months immediately after the end of World War II, shelter, clothes, fuel, even food were in short supply in Berlin. People wandered the streets looking for a job or something they could salvage from the ruins and sell.

One day a young woman was scavenging in a bombed out apartment building when she bumped into a man. She was about to shout to tell him to watch where he was going, but she stopped herself. The man wore very dark glasses and held a long white cane in his hand. The poor man was blind.

"I am so sorry," the woman said. "I should be more careful."

"There's no harm done," the blind man assured her. And so they fell to talking.

"Could I ask you to do a small favor me? Would you mind delivering this letter? You will have an easier time finding the address than I will," the blind man asked after a few minutes.

The woman looked at the address on the envelope. It wasn't too far out of her way.

"Yes," she said. "I can deliver this for you."

"You are very kind," the blind man said. "Now if you will excuse me, I have an appointment."

The young woman watched as the blind man made his way slowly through the crowd. After he had inched his way to a street corner, he suddenly began to run, and as he ran he stuffed his dark glasses into his coat pocket and folded up his white cane.

Suspicious, the young woman looked for a policeman and showed him the letter.

"A man I thought was blind asked me to deliver this for him," the woman said. "But then from the way he ran off it was obvious that he was not blind."

"Let's go to the address and see what happens," the policeman said. He called for help, and with half a dozen police officers the woman went to the mysterious address.

The woman stood at the curb while the policemen surrounded the house. A strange looking man opened the door. When he saw all the police he tried to run, but the officers arrested him. They searched the house, and in freezers in the cellar they found slabs of human flesh, wrapped in butcher's paper and priced for sale.

Out on the street, the policeman opened the envelope and took out the note.

"This is the last one I'm sending you today. Treat her like the rest," it read.

Oh, Susannah

Maggie and Sally were roommates at a college in Arkansas. Maggie was outgoing, while Sally was shy. When the drama department announced auditions for a school musical, Maggie tried out. She got a part singing the folk song, "Oh, Susannah."

Every night Maggie went off to rehearsal while Sally stayed in their dorm room studying. Maggie took her role so seriously that she practiced singing "Oh, Susannah" at every opportunity. The other girls on Maggie's floor were pretty tired of hearing the song night after night, but Sally never said a word about it.

Finally the night of play arrived. Maggie begged Sally to come and see her, but Sally wouldn't commit herself.

"I have a lot of reading to do this weekend," she said.

Maggie's performance wasn't quite the huge hit she had hoped it would be. In spite of all her practice, her voice cracked on stage.

The poor girl was humiliated.

After the play, Maggie skipped the cast party and went back to her room. The lights were out when she arrived, and she didn't want to turn them on in case Sally was sleeping.

As she started to undress in the dark, Maggie heard Sally's rocking chair creak.

"Sally? Why are you sitting here in the dark."

From the direction of the rocking chair a husky voice began to sing, "Oh, Susannah, don't you cry for me...."

"Don't be mean, Sally," Maggie said. "I've had a rough night."

But the voice sang again, "Oh, Susannah, don't you cry for me...."

"This isn't funny. Now knock it off."

Once again the voice sang, "Oh, Susannah, don't you cry for me...."

"All right, Sally, stop it!" And Maggie switched on the light.

There was Sally's body, rocking slowly in the chair. But her severed head was sitting on the little table under the window. And standing behind the chair, holding an enormous knife dripping with blood, was an insane looking man.

Maggie screamed.

"Help! Someone please help me!"

"There's no one here," the killer said. "Everyone went to see you in the play. I went too."

Maggie began to cry.

"Please don't hurt me. Please let me go. I won't tell anyone about you."

Maggie tried to edge toward the door, but the killer tackled her and pinned her to the floor. Maggie was screaming and weeping uncontrollably.

The killer sang, "Oh, Susannah, don't you cry for me...." as he sliced off Maggie's head.

THE PHANTOM CAR
AND OTHER
SUPERNATURAL ENCOUNTERS

THE PHANTOM CAR

On a snowy night in 1930 in Lancaster, Pennsylvania, a farm family heard a car coming up the lane toward their house. As they gathered on the porch to see who could be visiting them, a sleek black Rolls Royce drove slowly past the house and headed for the barn. There the car stopped and a tall man dressed all in black climbed out of the Rolls, opened the double doors and then drove the car inside. For a moment, the interior of the barn was illuminated by the car's head lights, then all was dark again.

The father and the two oldest boys took lanterns and a shotgun to confront the trespasser. When they got to the barn, it was empty. There was no sign of the car, not even tire tracks in the snow.

Confused and frightened, the family got very little sleep that night. The next day, however, they forgot all about the strange event of the night before. The oldest son, who had gone out to the barn with his father and younger brother, had become deathly ill. He died before the doctor could get out to the farm.

The mother and father took the loss of their 17-year-old boy very hard. The mother confided to close relatives and friends that she believed the phantom car was a bad omen.

The months rolled by and soon it was winter again. The anniversary of the oldest boy's death came and went and the memory of the mysterious visitor had faded. One snowy night, the family heard the sound of a car driving up their lane. They collected on the porch and saw the same Rolls Royce heading slowly through the snow for the barn.

The father shouted at the driver to stop, but the car did not even slow down. At the barn, the driver dressed all in black climbed out, opened the barn doors and then drove the Rolls Royce inside. The father and his oldest surviving boy ran across the yard and reached the barn doors just as the car's headlights switched off. But there was no Rolls Royce in the barn, and no trace of it in the snow.

The next morning, the boy who had gone to the barn with his father was stricken with the same mysterious illness that had carried off his older brother. And like his brother, the 16-year-old boy died before the doctor could get out to the farm.

Now the whole family was terribly frightened. The mother wanted to sell the farm and move into town, but the father refused. Instead, they invited their pastor to come pray over them and bless the farm.

When winter came again, the whole family was anxious, especially on snowy nights. But no phantom car appeared that winter or that spring, or summer. Perhaps the pastor's blessing had driven off the curse.

Then one autumn evening when it was still warm enough to keep the windows open, the family heard a car driving up their lane. They didn't go out on the porch. They didn't go out to the barn. They knew who it was.

All night the entire family sat up, the mother, the father, the four surviving children. When morning came, they were all very tired, but they were well. No one had fallen ill during the night.

After breakfast, the father went out to the fields. An hour or so later, one of the hired men ran into the kitchen. The father had gotten caught in the combine. The machine chewed off both his arms. In a matter of minutes he had bled to death.

After the funeral, the mother sold the farm, auctioned off the machinery and the livestock, and moved her children to her sister's house in town. After they had settled in, the woman realized she had left her box of family photographs at the farmhouse. So she borrowed her brother-in-law's car and drove alone back to the farm.

The box of photographs was where she had left them on the floor of her now-empty bedroom. As she picked up the box and headed for the stairs, she heard the familiar sound of a Rolls Royce driving up the lane.

Hours went by and still the mother did not return to her sister's house. As it grew dark, the family began to worry. They borrowed a neighbor's car and drove out to the farm. There was no sign of the woman in the house, or in the garden, or in the yard. At last they found her in the barn, clutching her box of family photographs. Dead.

The Ghost Children

Many years ago in San Antonio, Texas, a school bus full of children stalled on railroad tracks. As the driver tried to get the engine to turnover, a freight train at top speed raced down the track, smashed into the bus and killed the driver and all the children.

A few weeks after the tragedy, a car full of kids from the local high school stalled on the same railroad tracks. The boys were about to climb out of the car and push when everyone felt the car begin to rock gently forward. Then it glided over the tracks and rolled to safety on the other side.

The story spread throughout San Antonio. People began to drive to the railroad tracks and purposely cut the engine. Every time, the car rolled off the tracks to safety.

Finally a detective on the city's police force decided to conduct a little experiment. He dusted the entire surface of his car with the same powder he used at crime scenes to collect fingerprints. Then he drove to the railroad tracks and turned off his engine. Almost immediately he felt his car rocking gently, then it glided over the tracks.

When it stopped, the detective jumped out to examine the body of the car. In the powder on the rear and along the sides he saw the little handprints of dozens of children.

Variant: In Franklin Lakes, New Jersey, a similar story is told of the ghosts of teenagers who were killed when they ran a stop sign at the bottom of an exit off Route 208. Drivers that edge past the sign feel invisible hands pushing their car back up the exit.

The Baby's Bridge

One frigid Christmas night many years ago, after spending the holiday with their family, a young mother and father and their one-year-old baby set out for home.

The roads were slick with ice, but the husband drove slowly. When they reached the tollbooth of the Bear Mountain Bridge over the Hudson River, the toll collector warned them that the ice was especially thick on the bridge.

"Can't you folks take another route?" the toll collector said.

"Our house is only five miles on the other side," the husband said. "I'll be careful going across."

But the ice on the surface of the bridge was more treacherous than the family imagined. The tires couldn't get a grip on the road. The rear of the car shimmied dangerously. Anxious, even desperate to get off the bridge, the husband leaned heavily on the gas pedal.

The car shot forward then spun out of control before it crashed through the railings and plunged into the Hudson River far below.

The next day, the bodies of the mother and father were found washed up on the shore a mile down river. The car was discovered and hauled out of the water a day or two later. The baby, however, was not inside. For a week, police divers worked in the terrible winter weather trying to find the infant's body. But it was never recovered.

Ever since that terrible Christmas, travelers who cross the Bear Mountain Bridge on a cold winter night say that they can hear the wailing of an infant.

The Sisters' Bridge

The Swarkestone Bridge in England stretches almost a mile across the River Trent. The first bridge on the site was erected in the 13th century by two sisters of a noble family.

The story goes that both young women were engaged to marry. Their future husbands were handsome young barons, and everyone expected that the double wedding would be a splendid affair. The day before the ceremony, the two young men waded across the Trent to attend a conference of local landowners. The meeting dragged on until after dark. By that time the tide was in and the current in the Trent was stronger and swifter than it had been that morning. Yet the bridegrooms insisted that they would return to their brides that night. They urged their horses into the swift-flowing stream, but neither man ever made it to the other side. The horses and their riders all drowned in the powerful current of the River Trent.

The tragedy broke the sisters' hearts. They vowed that they would never marry and they would use their dowries to build a bridge across the Trent.

It is said that on stormy nights when the river is high and the current is strong, you can see two ghostly young women weeping as they walk back and forth across the bridge, looking over the railing into the water for their lost lovers.

The Fisherman

The Nolichucky River in Tennessee is notorious for its treacherous undertow and the unseen underwater pits and caverns that have taken the lives of many swimmers and fishermen who waded too far out into the current. Some of the old folks tell of a fisherman from up North who went down to the Nolichucky to do a little fishing and never returned. The story goes that he appears on the river from time to time.

A few years back, a party of rafters in search of whitewater was drifting down the Nolichucky when they saw a fisherman standing waist-deep in the river. The rafters waved to the fisherman, and he waved back. Then, inexplicably, the fisherman disappeared.

Thinking the fisherman must have fallen victim to one of the underwater chasms, the leader of the expedition ordered the rafters to paddle over to the place where the man had been standing. As the raft drew near the spot, the guide pulled off his shirt and shoes and dove into the river. As he suspected, he found a large hole, the mouth of an underwater cave. After a moment's hesitation, the guide swam in, feeling his way in the semi-darkness. Up ahead of him he saw a flash of white and he swam for it, hoping it was the lost fisherman. What the guide found when he reached the spot was a human skull.

Frightened, the guide gave no more thought to the fisherman, but swam as fast he could out of the cave. He shot to the surface and dragged himself onto the riverbank where he lay gasping for air.

A few hours later, police divers brought up the skull and the rest of a human skeleton. They also found an old pair of wadders and the remnants of a wicker creel.

The congregation of a local church gave the bones a Christian burial in their burial ground. Since that day, the ghostly fisherman never appeared at the river again.

The Checker Cab

A cabbie with 10 years experience driving the night shift got a call to go to Red Hook, a part of Brooklyn where he had never been before. It was 4 a.m. as he drove down the deserted streets of the unfamiliar neighborhood, looking for his fare. Suddenly, as he rounded a corner, a man came running out of an alley. The cab hit the runner broadside. He flipped onto the hood of the cab and for a few brief seconds clung to the windshield wipers and looked the cabbie straight in the eye. Then the man rolled off the hood onto the pavement.

The cabbie slammed on the brakes and jumped out of his cab. He expected to find the man lying in the gutter, but there was no one anywhere on the street. The cabbie inspected his car for damage, but there wasn't a scratch on it. Nor were there any handprints on the glass where the man had grabbed the windshield wipers.

At the end of his shift, back at the garage, the cabbie told his friends what had happened to him that night. No one believed him.

A week later, a different cabbie was driving down the same street at the same unholy hour when a man ran out from an alley directly into the path of the cab. When the driver got out to help, the man had vanished. The cabbie went back to the garage and told his story. Again, none of the other drivers believed him.

Yet week after week, drivers showed up at the end of the night shift telling the same story. Now, the laughing and hooting had stopped. The cabbies were definitely spooked.

Finally, the dispatcher decided to do a little research. He called up a friend at *The Daily News* and asked him to search for any accidents in Red Hook in which a man had been hit by a cab in the early hours of the morning.

A few days later, the reporter called back. A Red Hook man had indeed been struck by a cab and killed at the very intersection where the cabbies reported seeing him. The victim had been trying to get away from an angry drug dealer when he ran into the path of the cab, was struck and killed.

"Did this happen about eight weeks ago?" the dispatcher asked.

"No," said his friend at the News. "It happened five years ago."

The Ghosts of the S.S. Watertown

In the 1920s, a cargo ship was steaming across the Atlantic from England to Canada. A few days out from Southhampton, a gas pipe in the cargo hold developed a tiny leak. The two crewmen who were assigned to keep the hold in good order died from inhaling the toxic fumes. That same day they were buried at sea.

The morning after the funeral when the captain came on deck he found his entire crew gathered at the stern, pointing at the ship's wake.

"What's going on here," the captain demanded of the first mate.

"Sir, it appears that the two men we buried yesterday are following the ship."

The captain looked at his first mate as if the man had lost his mind.

"Look for yourself, sir," the first mate said.

Although he felt foolish, the captain did look where the first mate pointed. To his horror, he could see the ghostly figures of both crewmen, floating above the wake of the ship.

"Who has a camera?" the captain said. "Bring it here immediately."

The ship's surgeon ran to his cabin, returning a few minutes later with a fine German camera.

"I want you to use all your film," the captain ordered. "We may all be suffering from mass hysteria. Or this may be a peculiar natural phenomenon. Whatever it is, I want a photographic record that can be investigated when we reach port."

The ship's surgeon did as he was ordered and took 24 shots of the ghostly figures.

Several days later, the Watertown docked in Halifax. The surgeon was the first man off the ship. Under orders from the captain, he hurried to a photographer's studio and asked him to develop the film at once. After he told the story of the apparitions, the surgeon also insisted that he be permitted to witness the entire developing process.

The ship surgeon's story of the ghosts intrigued the photographer. He put aside all his other work to develop this one roll of film.

In the dark room, frame after frame emerged from the developing solution perfectly black. "You must have gotten a bad roll," the photographer said. "Too bad. I would like to see a ghost."

Then he lifted the final frame out of the basin. It was a perfectly clear photograph of the wake of the ship. And floating above the sea were the transparent figures of the two dead sailors.

The Haunted Bar

In the Greenwich Village neighborhood of New York City is a small bar in an old red brick rowhouse. Two hundred years ago, the property was owned by Aaron Burr. Whenever the bar's owner hired a new bartender or waitress, the rest of the staff always told the rookie that the place was haunted.

"Never go into the store room after midnight," they told the new employees. "That's where the ghost hangs out."

One young woman who took a job as a waitress at the bar was not impressed by ghost stories. No matter what horrors the rest of the staff told her, she wasn't buying it.

Late one Saturday night in summer, after she had been working at the bar for only a few weeks, the waitress went into the storeroom to get some pretzels. When she flipped on the light, she saw a man in an antique costume standing among the boxes.

"Who are you?" she said. "What are you doing back here?"

The man looked the waitress straight in the eye.

"Where is Theodora?"

The waitress frowned. "Nobody named Theodora works here. Now get out."

But the man didn't move. He repeated his question.

"Where is Theodora?"

"Are you high?" the waitress said. "I told, there's no Theodora here. Now get out before I call the bouncer."

Now the man wailed, "Where is Theodora?"

Thinking this nut case might be dangerous, the waitress backed out of the store room and ran for the bouncer.

"There's a guy dressed up in weird old clothes in the store room. He wants some chick named Theodora," she told the bouncer. "Do you want to handle this, or should I call the cops?"

"Cops don't arrest ghosts," the bouncer said.

"What are you talking about," the waitress said.

"You just saw Aaron Burr's ghost," the bouncer said. "He's looking for his daughter, Theodora. She was lost at sea."

The Ghostly Handprint

This legend is one of the most famous ghost stories in the city of Chicago.

On an April day in the 1920s, a fireman named Frank Leavy was washing the windows at his firehouse. While he washed the glass, he chatted with a fellow firefighter. Suddenly, Frank put down his wash rag, leaned his hand against the glass window pane.

"You know, I just had a strange premonition that I would die today," he said to his friend.

At that moment, the station's alarm went off. Frank left his bucket and wash rags and ran for the fire truck. Soon Frank and dozens of other Chicago firefighters were battling a blaze at a huge downtown office building. In the middle of the battle, a wall collapsed, killing eight firemen. Frank Leavy was among the dead.

The next day, Frank's friend saw something odd on one of the station house's window panes. It was the imprint of a hand, and it was on the exact spot where Frank had been leaning the day before, the place where he predicted that he would die.

The firemen tried every cleaning solution on the market to remove the imprint, but nothing worked. When the story of the indelible hand print spread around the city, an expert from a Chicago glass manufacturer guaranteed the fire department that he remove the stain. But he failed.

Some of the firefighters argued that the glass pane was bad luck and it should be removed, but Frank's friends at the firehouse—and he had lots of them—said it would be disrespectful to the dead to take the window away.

For more than 20 years, the ghostly handprint remained intact at the fire house, until one morning a paperboy made a bad throw with the newspaper and shattered the mysterious window.

The Naked Ghost of the Rue Royale

Several decades before the start of the Civil War a woman of mixed race who was a slave in a fine house on New Orleans' Rue Royale fell desperately in love with her master. One day she dared to confess her love and begged her master to make her his wife.

A cruel master might have killed the slave for such boldness, or at least sold her off, but this man did not have a harsh disposition. He did not even want to hurt the poor woman's feelings. So he thought he would set an impossible condition that the woman would not even consider performing.

"If you spend an entire winter's night naked on the roof of the house," the master said, "I will marry you."

The woman went away heart-broken and never spoke of marriage to her master again.

During the week before Christmas, the master invited a friend over for a game of chess. It was a damp, cold night for New Orleans. While the men played before a warm fire, the lovelorn slave woman stripped off all her clothes and climbed onto the roof of the house. There she stayed all night long. And that's where the other house slaves found her the next morning—naked, cold as ice, and dead.

For his part, when the master learned that his little jest had cost the woman her life. He went mad.

Today, residents of the Rue Royale say that on cold December nights, they still see the slave woman standing naked on the roof, while the master fills the house with cries of despair.

The Dead Lover's Advice

A young New Orleans couple fell in love in the weeks before the United States entered World War I. They planned to marry. But when the war broke out, the young man enlisted. He promised his fiancee that they be married when he came home.

Faithfully, every week, the young woman received a letter from her husband-to-be. Then there was a week when no letter came. One week stretched to three and then to six weeks without any news from the boy. Finally, the young woman learned from her fiancee's mother that he had been badly wounded in France. The Army was shipping him home.

The long journey back to New Orleans proved to be too much

for the poor soldier. He died less than a week after his return.

The young woman could not be consoled. She went to the dead man's grave everyday and sat there for hours. She said her dead lover communicated with her.

A year after the soldier's death, the young woman met a stranger to New Orleans. He was rich, handsome, and he pursued her with a passion she had never known before. Then the wealthy stranger asked the young woman to marry him. She didn't know what to say. She was still mourning her first love. So she asked for time to consider the proposal.

That night the woman went to the soldier's grave. She sat on the bench opposite the headstone.

"There's a newcomer in town who wants to marry me," she said. "He's very successful, good-looking, he appears to love me very much. But I don't know if I should accept his proposal. We know so little about him, and I am still so sad that I lost you. Tell me what I should tell him."

Now, planted on either side of the dead soldier's headstone were rose bushes, one red, the other white. It was winter, the flowers had all faded away months before, yet now the two bushes burst into bloom. Fourteen buds appeared on the red bush, fifteen on the white. The woman collected the flowers, held them in her lap, counting them over and over again as she wondered what the message signified.

Then it came to her: the fourteenth letter of the alphabet is N, the fifteenth is O. Her dead fiancee had sent her an answer.

Soon after the young woman refused the stranger's offer of marriage, he left town. Months later the story came back that he was already married—to three different women, in three different parts of the South.

Laura

A visitor to Alexandria, Virginia took a walk through the historic Old Town. At one point, she wandered into a lovely old house that had been converted to a Christmas shop. She selected a few ornaments and some other Christmas decorations and took them to the counter.

While the cashier rang up the woman's purchase, the shopper felt a cold draft rush past her. Then she thought she heard a woman screaming. She looked around, but there was no one else in the store other than herself and the clerk.

"Don't be concerned," the cashier said.

"What do you mean?" the shopper said.

"You felt a cold wind and you heard a woman screaming, didn't you?"

"Yes! Did you feel it and hear it, too?"

"I experience it at least three times a day. It's Laura," the clerk said. "Do you have time to hear an old story?"

"Absolutely," the woman said.

"Well, about a 150 years ago, this house belonged to a prominent family. Their daughter, Laura, was engaged to be married. On her wedding day she was dressed and ready to go to church when she brushed too close to a candle flame. Before she knew what had happened, her dress caught fire. In panic, she ran out of her bedroom. By the time she reached this staircase she a ball of fire. She was dead before she reached the bottom.

"As I said, Laura's ghost races through the shop several times a day. Some folks say she is trying to get to the river to extinguish the fire. But her ghost never leaves this old house," the sales clerk said. "Perhaps if she could get to the water her soul would know some peace."

The Blue Light

This story originates in Ohio.

In the first years of the 20th century, a young woman named Nora fell in love with a young man who was good-looking and ambitious but nonetheless selfish and cruel. Her family and friends warned Nora to give him up, but the young woman insisted that she could change him.

They had been dating for a few months when Nora discovered

that her beau was cheating on her with a woman in a neighboring town. They had a tremendous fight. Everyone was certain that the love match was over. But the next day, Nora and her bad boy were still a couple.

The Saturday night after their quarrel, Nora and her man walked out to an old covered bridge. They kissed in the shadows beneath the bridge. Then the boyfriend stretched out and fell asleep with his head in Nora's lap. As he dozed, Nora took a long sharp knife from her purse and slit her lover's throat.

Then she lifted the knife again and cut her own throat.

When a fisherman found the two bloody corpses the next day, Nora still had her fingers wrapped in her cheating lover's hair.

The old wooden bridge is long gone and a new, concrete one stands in its place. But if you stand on the bridge after midnight and call Nora's name, a blue light will appear down by the stream and slowly make its way up to the bridge.

The Boy in the Bleachers

After a long day, a guidance counselor at a high school in rural Indiana decided to hit the gym before he went home. It after 8 p.m. All the teachers, students and staff had gone home long ago.

In the boys' locker room the counselor changed into a T-shirt, shorts and running shoes, then he sprinted up the stairs to the gym.

He had done a few laps around the gym when he noticed a boy standing at the top of the bleachers watching him. The counselor waved as he ran by and shouted hello, but the boy didn't respond.

For the next half hour while the counselor worked out the boy never left his spot on the bleachers. He did not even change his facial expression. The counselor was beginning to feel uneasy. Maybe the kid was on something and needed a doctor. He stopped running and walked toward the bleachers to confront the kid, but the boy was gone.

The counselor was searching for the boy when he met one of the school's custodians.

"Have you seen a boy around here tonight?" the counselor asked.

"No," the custodian said. "Have you?"

"Yeah. I was doing laps in the gym when I spotted this kid standing on the top of bleachers watching me," the counselor said. "He was as still as a statue. I thought I'd ask him if he needed some help, or a ride home, but the moment I started walking toward the bleachers, the kid disappeared. I've been looking for him everywhere. I don't suppose you saw him?"

"You won't find that boy," the custodian said. "He's long gone."

"Then you saw him leave the building?"

"Nope. But I saw him die."

The counselor was speechless.

"At a basketball game in the gym, Mike Horgan fell off the topmost bleacher and split his head open. He was dead before anyone got to him. That was twenty-five years ago this very night. Mike always comes back to the gym for an hour or so on the anniversary."

The Bloody Angel

In an old graveyard in Baltimore stands the statue of an angel. The sculpture marks a double grave. The first body buried there was a 9-year-old girl who was murdered by her own mother. It was the child's grief-stricken relatives who erected a large sculpture of an angel over the little girl.

Meanwhile, the mother was tried, convicted and sentenced to life in prison. For the next 10 years, she was a model of the repentant sinner. She wrote letter after letter to her family begging them to forgive her. She became a devout Christian. She volunteered to work in the prison hospital where she performed the most unpleasant tasks cheerfully.

Then one morning the matron found the woman dead in her cell.

Now the family faced a dilemma? Where should they bury this woman? Some argued that she should be buried in the prison cemetery. Others insisted because the woman had shown every sign of sorrow for her crime, she ought to be buried beside the child she killed. In the end, the family agreed to bury the woman in the same plot with her dead daughter.

Aside from the large crowd that gathered around the statue of the angel, the woman's burial service was no different than any other. When the final prayer had been said, the pallbearers lowered the coffin into the grave. As it came to rest at the bottom, the entire crowd could hear the distinct sound of droplets striking the coffin's wooden lid. The mourners looked up to see if it was beginning to rain, but the sky was clear and the sun was bright. Then the dead woman's sister pointed at the angel.

"She has blood on her hands!" she shrieked.

The angel's hands were indeed red with blood, which trickled off the sculpture's fingertips and struck the coffin of the little girl's killer.

How the Modern World Went to Hell

It's said that beneath the Vatican are vast catacombs that serve as storage areas for strange artifacts, forgotten sacred objects and bogus relics.

One day in 1914, a novice monk was pestering an elderly monsignor with questions about the "secrets of the Vatican."

"There are no secrets anymore," the old priest said. "Every document in the Archive, every book and manuscript in the library, every work of art in the museums has been catalogued."

But the novice persisted.

"That can't be true. There must be some things that were overlooked."

The old man sighed. It was past noon and he wanted his lunch. More to the point, he wanted this chatty, irritating, would-be monk to leave him in peace.

"Yes. There is one place that is still secret. The ancient cellars of the Vatican are filled with peculiar objects that have not seen the sunlight in centuries. Adam's rib is said to be down there, and a feather from the wings of the Angel Gabriel and no less than 27 skulls, all purporting to be the true head of St. John the Baptist."

"It sounds wonderful!" the novice said.

"You would think so. But other objects are down there, too, things that should remain hidden and forgotten. You're too curious, boy. It will only get you into trouble."

But the novice begged and pleaded to be allowed to explore the storage rooms. Finally, the monsignor relented.

"Go to the Security Office. Tell Fabrizio I said he should open the door for you."

"Oh! Thank you monsignor!"

"Good. Fine. Enjoy yourself," the old man said as he walked

away.

An hour later, the novice was wandering happily through the storage area. The old monsignor had been right, most of what the novice saw was junk. But then he spotted something out of the ordinary.

In a cabinet all by itself was a clay jar of great age. The novice held his lamp closer to the ancient jar and saw a label which read "Tenebrae Aegypti"—the Darkness of Egypt. Below the heading was this verse from the Book of Exodus, "And the Lord said to Moses: Stretch out thy hand towards heaven: and may there be darkness upon the Land of Egypt, so thick it may be felt. And Moses stretched forth his hand towards heaven: and there came horrible darkness."

A shiver of terror ran up the novice's spine. The jar slipped from his grasp, shattering on the filthy stone pavement. From the fragments rose a dense black cloud that began to spread through the catacomb.

With a cry of horror the novice ran for the door, slammed it and locked it behind him. But the dark cloud seeped out from under the door and through every crack in the wood.

Once again the novice took to his heels, running back the way he came, up through the catacombs, through the sub-basements and cellars of the Vatican, back to the light of day and the crowded, noisy streets of Rome. Yet he felt no relief when he stood in the sunlight.

He knew the darkness would spread over the city, perhaps over the whole world and there was nothing the novice could do to stop it.

Within a few weeks, the novice saw the first sign that the supernatural darkness was at work. First came the horrors of World War I and then the bloody chaos of the Russian Revolution. This was followed by the rise of Stalin and then Hitler, World War II, the dropping of the atomic bomb, the Communist take-over in China. Year after year the monk saw bloodshed, hatred, and the collapse of the old social order.

And he knew it was all his fault.

THE NAVY PILOT'S
COLLISION COURSE AND
OTHER ON-THE-JOB FOIBLES

THE NAVY PILOT'S COLLISION COURSE

A Navy fighter pilot was out on a routine test flight along the coast of New England when a heavy fog set in. Suddenly, straight ahead of him, the pilot saw a light.

"Change your course. You are endangering us both," he radioed to the approaching plane.

He heard a man's voice over the radio.

"No. It's up to you to change your course."

The Navy pilot was furious. Who was this idiot?

"Look, buddy," he said, "do realize that you're talking to the U.S. Navy?"

"And do you realize that you're flying straight into the Cape Neddick Lighthouse?"

The Backyard Archaeologist

Scott Williams of Vermont is an amateur archaeologist whose backyard has proven to be a treasure trove of rare artifacts, all of which he donates to the Smithsonian. After his latest bequest, Williams received this reply from one of the museum's curators.

Smithsonian Institute
207 Pennsylvania Avenue
Washington, DC 20078

Dear Mr. Williams:

Thank you for your latest submission to the Institute, labeled "93211-D, layer seven, next to the clothesline post...Hominid skull." Naturally, we have given this specimen a careful and detailed examination. After reviewing the lab report, it is my sad duty to inform you that we cannot concur with your theory that the skull is conclusive proof that Early Man was living in Vermont 12 million years ago.

Rather, it appears that what you have found is the head of a Barbie doll. We consulted a specialist in this field, Tiffany DiStefano, the seven-year-old daughter of one of our curators. Miss DiStefano informs me that the head belongs to "Malibu Barbie," and can be dated no earlier than 1995.

All of us at the museum respect the effort you expended analyzing this specimen. Those of us who are familiar with your prior work in the field were loath to contradict your findings. Nonetheless, we feel compelled to highlight several physical attributes of the specimen which might have tipped you off to its modern origin:

1. The material is molded plastic. Ancient hominid remains

are fossilized bone.

2. The cranial capacity of the specimen is approximately 9 cubic centimeters, well below the threshold of even the earliest identified proto-hominids.

3. The bite pattern found on the skull is more consistent with the common domesticated dog than it is with the ravenous man-eating Pliocene clams you speculate roamed the wetlands of southern Vermont 12 million years ago.

All of us at the Smithsonian were especially intrigued by your man-eating clams hypotheses. Alas, in your zeal for science you overlooked a minor but telling point: clams don't have teeth.

It is with feelings tinged with melancholy that we must deny your request to have the specimen carbon-dated. Our reasons are twofold. Surely you can appreciate the heavy burden our lab must bear in its normal operation, and to the best of our knowledge, no Barbie dolls were produced prior to 1956.

We must also deny your request to assign your specimen the scientific name "Australopithecus spiff-arino."

While I, and several others, fought tenaciously on your behalf, in the end the committee voted down your proposal. They explained that common usage within the scientific community bars species names that are hyphenated. Furthermore, the committee members felt that Australopithecus spiff-arino didn't really sound much like Latin.

I do have some good news for you. We are pleased to accept your generous donation of this fascinating specimen to the museum. It is yet another riveting example of the great body of work you have accumulated here. You should know that our Director has reserved a special shelf in his own office for the display of the specimens you have previously submitted to the Institution, and the entire staff speculates daily on what you will happen upon next in your digs in your back yard.

We eagerly anticipate your trip to our nation's capital, and several of us are pressing the Director to pay for your travel expenses. We are particularly interested in hearing you expand upon your theories regarding the trans-positating fillifitation of ferrous ions in a structural matrix that makes the excellent juvenile Tyrannosaurus rex femur you recently discovered take on the deceptive appearance of a rusty 9-mm Sears Craftsman automotive crescent wrench.

Yours in Science,
Harvey Rowe, Chief Curator–Antiquities

Airborne Chickens

Early in its career, the Royal Canadian Air Force had suffered several casualties when birds collided with an aircraft's windshield. To test the strength of newly designed windshields, the RCAF developed a device that shot a chicken carcass at the glass at the usual speed of the aircraft. If the windshield didn't break, then it was likely that the plane would survive any midair collision with birds.

When officials of the FAA in the United States heard about this device, they were impressed and asked their Canadian colleagues to come down and show them how to conduct the test.

The first test took place at Andrews Air Force Base. The Canadian engineers positioned their device in front of a fighter plane. The Americans loaded the chicken carcass into the barrel of the device and set the discharge to an American fighter plane's maximum speed. Then they fired.

The chicken carcass was hurled out of the devise, shattered the windshield, smashed through the headrest of the pilot's seat, and embedded itself into the rear wall of the cockpit.

"I don't understand," the chief FAA engineer said to the Canadians. "What did we do wrong?"

"Well," the Canadian engineer said, "Next time you might want to let the chicken thaw."

Built in a Day

Stories about difficult American tourists are more than a century old. One of the classic examples comes from Mark Twain's comic novel, Innocents Abroad (1869), in which American travelers to Italy torment their guide by pretending that they are not impressed by anything they see.

A cab driver in Rome picked up an American tourist in front of the Hassler Hotel. "I've never been to Rome before," the American said, "so how about driving me around and pointing out the most important sights."

"Sure. Okay. No problem," the cabbie said.

First he drove to the Colosseum. "Wow! That's impressive," the American said. "How long did it to take to built the Colosseum?"

"Oh, maybe three, four years," the cabbie said.

"Really? That long? In the States we could have that up in a little over a year. And we'd have Sky Boxes."

The cab driver was silent.

Next he pulled up in front of the Pantheon. "This is an intact Roman temple. The dome is the largest ever built in the ancient world."

"Beautiful," the American said. "How long did it take the emperors to build this temple?"

"No more than two years. They worked very fast," the driver said.

"That's not so fast. For a little thing like this our contractors back home would be done in under a year."

Now the cabbie was beginning to get angry. So he drove the

American to St. Peter's Basilica.

"Spectacular!" the American said. "What is this church called?"

"I don't know," the cabbie said. "It was not here this morning."

The Roughneck's Revenge

On an oil rig off the coast of Alaska, a roughneck, as members of the drilling crew are called, lost his grip on a twelve-pound sledge hammer and dropped it down a newly drilled oil well. Naturally the hammer wedged itself in the worst possible position so the pump would not operate. The rig's foreman had no choice but to call the mainland and have a repair crew bring equipment out to the rig to extract the hammer.

The whole procedure cost a small fortune, and it was two days before the hammer was finally dislodged. Once it was brought back up to the surface, the foreman handed the sledgehammer to the roughneck who'd dropped it in the first place and said, "Here. You're fired."

"Then I guess I won't need this anymore," said the roughneck as he tossed the hammer down the well again.

The Seventh Boy

Every afternoon, immediately before supper, the headmaster of a boy's school in northern England dealt with students who had broken the school regulations that day. He had an established routine. The miscreants lined up in the hallway outside the headmaster's office. The boys were ordered to hold out their hands, palms upward. Then the headmaster went down the line with a bamboo cane and gave each offender half a dozen sharp blows.

One day the headmaster stepped out of his office to find seven boys lined up and waiting.

"Assume the position," he ordered. All the boys extended their hands except for the tall boy at the end of the line.

When the headmaster got to him, he shouted, "I said assume the position."

The frightened boy could only stammer, "B-b-b-but...."

"Hold out your hands, damn you!"

Slowly the tall boy extended his hands. After the first blow of the cane, he snatched them back and began to cry.

"What's the matter with you, boy," the headmaster said. "And who are you? Why haven't I seen you before."

"I'm Willis, sir," the boy said.

"Don't be foolish. There is no Willis at this school."

"I don't go to the school, sir," the tall boy said. "I work at the telegraph office. I just came to deliver a telegram to you."

The Missing Co-Pilot

Halfway between a DC-9's flight from Miami to Washington, D.C., the co-pilot left the cockpit to use the bathroom. Fifteen minutes later he had not returned so the pilot called one of the flight attendants on the intercom and asked her to tap on the lavatory door to see if the co-pilot needed anything.

"Sorry, Captain," the flight attendant said. "We're in the middle of beverage service. The carts are blocking the aisles."

So the captain activated autopilot, stepped outside the cockpit and shut the door behind him.

At that moment, the co-pilot emerged from the bathroom.

"What are you doing out here?" he asked the pilot.

"You were gone an awfully long time. I wanted to make sure you weren't sick."

"I'm fine," the co-pilot said. "But the next time we're in Miami, remind me to stay away from refried beans. You got the key?"

The pilot was quiet for a moment. "No. I thought you had the key."

"Great. How do we get back in?"

"The important thing is not to panic the passengers," the co-pilot said. "Here. I've got an idea."

The co-pilot opened the compartment that held fire equipment and removed the ax. With one blow he smashed open the cockpit door.

The plane erupted in pandemonium as passengers screamed. "There are terrorists on the plane! They're going to kill the pilot!"

"Nice work," the captain said. "I can't wait to see the letters we get from the passengers about this flight."

Variants: the pilot is locked out when he leaves the cockpit to greet the passengers, or to get sugar for his coffee.

Dead Again

A funeral director received a call one rainy night from a man whose elderly mother had just died.

Within an hour, the director and one of his employees had driven to the man's home, removed the body and were returning it to the funeral home.

Suddenly they heard a gurgling sound from the back of the hearse. The employee gave the funeral director a quizzical look. "It's nothing. Just an air bubble escaping from the lungs. Happens all the time."

When the hearse went over several potholes and some railroad tracks, the two men heard a distinct groan. They pulled over, checked the woman, and found that she was alive. "Let's get to a hospital!" the funeral director said.

The driver of the hearse raced for the nearest emergency room, but bad roads and bad weather were working against him. He lost control of the hearse on a slick stretch of road. The car spun around and the rear half of the hearse smashed into a huge tree.

When an ambulance arrived a few minutes later, the paramedics found the driver and the funeral director alive but unconscious. But the woman in the back was dead.

The Jaws of Death

A dentist was working on an elderly patient's teeth when the man convulsed in the chair and died.

The panic-stricken dentist did something desperate. He locked the examination room door. Then he hoisted the dead man onto his shoulder, bounced the corpse up and down a few times to make sure he had a good grip on the body, and carried it out of the office the back way.

After staggering down several flights of stairs to the building maintenance crew's men's room, the dentist kicked open a stall door, dumped the dead man on the toilet, and then ran back up the stairs to the his private office.

While he was still trying to recover from his ordeal, his nurse came in. "Doctor, I thought you were treating Mr. Quincy, but he's the reception area. He says to tell you that was some weird CPR maneuver you used on him, but he's grateful that it worked."

The Butcher's Prank

A butcher saw a friend heading toward his shop, so he took a sausage and slipped into pants, letting the top two inches protrude over the top of his belt.

The friend entered the shop, ordered some steaks, some chicken breasts, and a roast. When the butcher came back from the freezer with the meat, his friend said, "Uh, Frank? Your equipment is showing."

Feigning surprise, the butcher glanced down at his crotch.

"Damn it! It always does that. I just can't take the embarrassment any more."

Then the butcher walked over the cutting board, opened his pants, laid the sausage on the board, grabbed a cleaver, and chopped off three inches of meat.

The shock was too much for the butcher's friend. He suffered a massive heart attack and dropped dead on the shop floor.

The friend's wife sued the butcher for $500,000—and won.

The Deadbeat Client

A stonemason spent three weeks building a beautiful fieldstone fireplace for a wealthy man in Greenwich, Connecticut. When the job was done, the mason presented the client with his bill.

"I'm a little embarrassed," the client said. "I forgot to go to the bank this morning. I don't have $5000 in cash on me."

"That's not a problem," the stonemason said. "I'll take a personal check."

"You know, I can't even do that," the wealthy man said. "I ran out of checks yesterday. It will be two weeks before the new set of checks arrive."

"Then I'll make a deal with you," the mason said. "If I have to wait for my money, you have to wait to use your new fireplace."

"Agreed," the client said. "I won't build a fire until I get you the money."

That night the stonemason received a phone call from his wealthy client. "Dammit! What the hell did you do? My house is full of smoke!"

"I told you not to use the fireplace until you paid me," the mason said.

"I have the money. I'll give you the full $5000 in cash," the client said. "Just get over here now and fix this!"

The stonemason found the rich man waiting on his front lawn. The doors and all the windows were wide open to air out the house.

"Have you got the money?" the stonemason asked.

"Yes. Here it is," the rich man said, as he handed the mason a large envelope. "Take it! Just fix the chimney."

The mason opened the envelope and counted the cash. The

full $5000 was there. Then he took a long aluminum ladder and a single red brick from the back of his truck. He leaned the ladder against the house, climbed to the top, and dropped the brick down the chimney. A moment later the two men heard the sound of shattering glass.

"What the hell was that?" the rich client said.

"That was my personal insurance policy," the stonemason said. "Whenever I build a chimney I mortar a pane of glass across the flue. If the client pays me right away, I break the glass before I leave the job. If the client tries to put me off... well, you know what happens then."

The Lipstick Mafia

Some of the cheerleaders at a middle school in Tennessee thought it was cute to crowd into the girls room, apply a fresh coat of lipstick, and then kiss the mirror to see who could leave the best lip prints.

The principal had scolded the girls for making a mess. "Do you have any idea how hard it is to get all that lipstick off half a dozen mirrors?" he said. But neither lectures nor detention made any impression on the cheerleaders. They started calling themselves "The Lipstick Mafia."

Late one Friday afternoon, after practice, the cheerleaders were back in the girls room indulging in their favorite little act of rebellion when a school custodian emerged from one of the stalls with a can of scouring cleanser in one hand and a toilet brush in the other. The girls were a little embarrassed to be caught in the act by the guy who had to clean-up after them.

The captain of the squad said, "You know, we're sorry we've made extra work for you. But why is it so hard to get lipstick off a mirror?"

"It was only tough in the beginning," the custodian said. "But for the past few months I've used this and it comes right off."

To demonstrate, he dipped the brush in the nearest toilet and scrubbed off the lip prints.

That was the last time the cheerleaders kissed the girls room mirrors.

The Soap Saga

A businessman checked into a fine hotel in Atlanta for a week-long stay. He traveled frequently and had gotten into the habit of bringing his own toiletries. He even carried along bath-size bars of favorite soap; he didn't like the soap hotels provided—the bars were too small and they made his skin break out. After his first night in the hotel, he left this note for the maid.

Dear Maid,

Please do not leave any more of those little bars of soap in my bathroom. I always bring my own soap. You will find three unopened little bars on the shelf under the medicine chest and another three in the shower soap dish. Please remove them. They are in my way.

Thank you,

Sam Berman

Dear Mr. Berman,

I am not the regular maid for your room. She had today off, but she will be back tomorrow. In the meantime, I removed the 3 hotel soaps from the shower soap dish as you requested. I moved the 3 bars from under your medicine chest and left them on top of your Kleenex dispenser in case you should change your mind. The hotel management requires us to leave 3 fresh bars of soap in each room every day. I hope this is satisfactory.

Kathy, Relief Maid

Dear Maid,

I hope you are my regular maid. Apparently Kathy, the relief maid, did not tell you about my note concerning the little bars of soap. When I got back to my room this evening I found you had added three little bars of soap to the shelf under my medicine cabinet. Now

I have six, but I don't want any of them. I always travel with my own soap. Furthermore, those six little bars of soap on the medicine chest shelf get in the way when I'm brushing my teeth and shaving. Please remove them. Thank you.

S. Berman

Dear Mr. Berman,

We are instructed by the management to bring 3 fresh bars of soap to each room every day. But since these soaps are in your way, I have moved them from the medicine cabinet shelf to the soap dish in the shower. Of course, I had to leave another 3 bars of soap, but I hid these inside your medicine cabinet. Please let me know if I can of further assistance.

Your regular maid,

Dotty

Dear Mr. Berman,

Mr. Davis, the hotel's assistant manager, informed me this morning that you called him last evening and said you were unhappy with your maid service. I have assigned a new girl to your room. I hope you will accept my apologies for any past inconvenience. If there is anything I can do to make your stay more pleasant, please call me directly at extension 1108 between 8AM and 5PM.

Thank you,
Elaine Carmen, Housekeeper

Dear Miss Carmen,
It is impossible to contact you by phone since I leave the hotel for business at 7:45 AM and don't get back before 6PM. That's the reason I called the assistant manager last night. You were already off duty. I only asked the assistant manager if he could waive housekeeping's policy of leaving little bars of soap in my room everyday. The new maid you assigned to my room apparently does not know about my notes to the two previous maids, Kathy and Dotty. She has left me three bars of soap in my shower and three more on the shelf under my medicine chest. I have accumulated 24 little bars of soap and I don't want any of them!
S. Berman

Dear Mr. Berman,
Your new maid, Michele, has been instructed to stop delivering soap to your room and remove the extra soaps. If I can be of further assistance, please call extension 1108 between 8AM and 5PM.
Thank you,
Elaine Carmen, Housekeeper

Dear Mr. Davis,

My personal bath-size bar of soap which I brought with me is missing. In fact, there was no soap in my room at all. I came in late last night and had to call the bellhop. He brought me 4 little Cashmere Bouquets.

S. Berman

Dear Mr. Berman,

I have informed our housekeeper, Elaine Carmen, of your soap problem. I cannot understand why there was no soap in your room since our maids are instructed to leave 3 bars of soap each time they service a room. The situation will be rectified immediately. Please accept my apologies for the inconvenience.

Martin L. Davis, Assistant Manager

Dear Mrs. Carmen,

Who the hell left 54 little bars of soap in my room? I came in last night and found 54 little bars of soap. I don't want them. All I want is the bath-size bar of soap I brought with me. Give me back my soap!

S. Berman

Dear Mr. Berman,

You complained of too much soap in your room so I had them removed. Then you complained to Mr. Davis that all your soap was missing so I personally returned the 24 bars which had been taken away by Michele plus the 3 bars you are supposed to receive daily. Obviously your maid did not know I had returned your soaps so she also brought 24 bars plus the 3 daily soaps. I don't know where you got the idea that this hotel issues bath-size bars of soap.

Elaine Carmen, Housekeeper

Dear Mrs. Camen,

Just a short note to bring you up-to-date on my latest soap inventory. As of today I possess:

• On the shelf under medicine cabinet, 18 bars in four stacks of four and one stack of two.

• On the Kleenex dispenser, 11 bars in two stacks of four and one stack of three.

• On the bedroom dresser, 1 stack of 3 Cashmere Bouquet, and eight additional bars of Cashmere Bouquet in two stacks of four.

• Inside the medicine cabinet, 14 bars in three stacks of four and one stack of two.

• In the shower soap dish, six bars, very moist.

• On the northeast corner of the bath tub, one Cashmere Bouquet, slightly used.

• On the northwest corner of the bath tub, six bars in two stacks of three.

Please ask Michele when she services my room to make sure the stacks are neatly piled and dusted. Also, please advise her that stacks of more than 4 have a tendency to tip. I would l like to point out that the window sill is empty and would make an excellent spot for future soap deliveries. One more item, I have purchased another bar of bath-sizcd of soap, which I am keeping in the hotel vault in order to avoid further misunderstandings.

S. Berman

The Penguin Fly-By

The Falkland Islands is one of the most boring assignments for pilots of the British Royal Air Force. After one of the pilots noticed that the thousands of penguins that inhabit the islands were fascinated by fighter jets, some of the Royal Air Force's top guns invented a unique game they called the Penguin Fly-By.

The pilots find the beach with the highest density of penguins and fly slowly just above the water's edge. The guys get a real kick watching thousand penguins slowly turn their heads in unison as they watch the planes go by.

When the pilots fly back, the birds turn their heads slowly in the opposite direction. One of the pilots has said its like seeing a stadium full of spectators at Wimbledon watching a slow-motion tennis match.

But the hot shots save the best part for last. They take the jets out to sea, turn around, and fly straight for the penguin colony. As they pass over the birds strain their necks to look up until ten thousand penguins topple over onto their backs.

A Bad Day at the Office

Dear Sue,

Yep, it's another note from your bottom-dwelling brother. Last week I had a really bad day at the office. I was testing a new device that would enable oceanographers like me to work at the bottom of the sea even in the coldest temperatures.

Here's how it works. On the dock of the ship we have a diesel-powered water heater. It sucks water out of the sea and heats it to the temperature of bath water. The warm water is pumped into the diver's wet suit through a very long hose.

It sounded like a good plan to me, so I put on my wet suit, attached the hose to the opening at the back of my neck, and went down. My whole suit was flooded with warm water. It was like working in a Jacuzzi. Everything was going great until my ass started to itch. Naturally, I scratched it. But within a few seconds my itchy ass started to burn. I'm not talking mild discomfort here; I mean someone's holding a flame-thrower set on high to my rectum.

In agony, I realized what had happened. The pump back on deck had sucked up a jellyfish and pumped it down the hose and into my suit. The little jellyfish had slid effortlessly down my smooth, hairless back and finally found a place to grab onto when it reached the definitely-not-hairless crack of my ass. By scratching I had actually driven the jellyfish further up my butt.

I radioed the dive supervisor of my situation and that I wanted to come up to the surface NOW. All I heard in response over the communications system was hysterical laughter.

Since I was instructed to make 3 hellish in-water decompression stops, it took over 35 minutes for me to reach the surface. When I climbed on board, the medic, with tears of laughter streaming down his face, handed me a tube of cream and told me to coat my ass when I got in the decompression chamber. The cream put the fire out, but I couldn't shit for two days because my asshole was swollen shut.

Since then we've modified the equipment to filter out sea creatures. And we've sent our recommendation to the manufacturer.

Anyway, the next time you have a bad day at the office, remember that it can't be as bad as squashing a jellyfish up your ass.

Your loving brother, Ned

I Know That Corpse!

Since this story was first published in London in 1896, it has been a perennial favorite in newspapers around the world. Variants have been collected from as far away as New Delhi.

A medical student at Johns Hopkins had a reputation for being completely cool in anatomy lab. The most gruesome dissection assignments, the most horribly mangled corpses of accident victims—nothing fazed this guy.

One morning, the medical student reported to the anatomy lab as usual. He pulled back the sheet, took one look at the body, and ran out of the room.

No one in the class could understand what had upset him. The body wasn't disfigured in any way.

After class, the medical student's lab partner tracked him down in a bar near campus. "What freaked you out in the lab today?" he asked. "There wasn't a thing wrong with the body."

"There was a lot wrong with that body," the medical student said. "I knew that guy. I hadn't seen him over five years, but I recognized him right away."

"That is freaky," his friend said. "What are the chances of getting an acquaintance's corpse as your lab assignment."

"He wasn't an acquaintance," the medical student said. "He was my father."

Variant: The medical student finds his mother on the dissecting table; she had disappeared a few weeks earlier.

Skylight Tanner

Playboy magazine featured this legend as a cartoon in the 1960s. In the 1990s, it was part of an episode of the Emmy-winning comedy, Frasier.

A woman from North Dakota decided to escape the frigid winter weather and take a vacation in Florida. The day she arrived, she explored her hotel and found that the roof had a wonderful view of the ocean.

That afternoon she put on her bikini, grabbed a towel, and headed for the roof to begin working on her tan. She had the place all to herself—no other guest of the hotel ventured up on the roof.

The next morning the woman went back to the roof again. By noon, after a morning of complete solitude, she was convinced that she had found the perfect place to get an all-over tan. She removed her bikini and stretched out in the warm Florida sun. But a few minutes later she heard the sound of footsteps hurrying up the stairs. She rolled over onto her stomach and threw the towel over her bottom.

A moment later the hotel's assistant manager stood before her, flustered and out of breath.

"I'm sorry, ma'am. You're welcome to sun yourself on the hotel roof, but we must insist that you wear your bathing suit."

"I can't see why," the woman said. "No one can see me up here."

"I'm afraid that's not true," the assistant manager said. "You're lying on the skylight over the restaurant."

The Concrete Tomb

At the turn of the 20th century, a new bridge was being constructed over the Ohio River. It was dangerous work and there were no safety regulations on the work site.

One blistering day in August, a man working on the framework where concrete was being poured for a massive pylon suffered a case of sunstroke, lost his footing, and plunged into the wet concrete. Before anyone could reach him, the workman sank without a trace.

The trustees who supervised the construction of the bridge rejected the idea of destroying the new pylon to recover the worker's body. It would cost tens of thousands of dollars and delay the work by several weeks. Instead, the board authorized a large payment to the dead man's wife and children and, under pressure from public opinion, agreed to place a small bronze plaque bearing the workman's name and the dates of his birth and death on the pylon in which he lies buried.

The plaque is still there to this day.

Home At Last

A British diplomat returned to England after 20 years of service in distant corners of the world. During his first week back in London, a member of the House of Lords invited the diplomat to a party.

The diplomat was mingling rather successfully when he came face to face with a woman who looked very familiar, but he could not recall her name. In an effort to get his bearings he said, "What a pleasure to see you again! How is your father."

"My father is dead," the woman replied.

"Oh, terribly sorry," the man said. "I've been away so long, I hadn't heard."

Still trying to get a clue who he was talking to the diplomat said, "Then how's your brother?"

"I don't have a brother," the woman said. "Just one sister."

"Of course, how stupid of me," the diplomat replied. "Now I remember. And what is your sister doing these days?"

"The same thing," the woman said. "She's still Queen."

THE HOTEL RESERVATIONIST AND OTHER TALES OF REVENGE

THE HOTEL RESERVATIONIST

An international hotel chain built a $10 million hotel outside Memphis. From the day the hotel opened for business, a woman who lived in the town began getting phone calls for the hotel—dozens of them, everyday. She appealed to the hotel management, but they refused to change their phone number, saying that they would have to alter all their advertisements, their stationery, and their listing in every hotel directory. The phone company would not help either. So the woman decided to take matters into her own hands.

The next time someone called and asked to book a room, she took the reservation. When a business executive called and requested a two-bedroom suite for seven nights, she offered him the Penthouse and quoted him a price of only $75 per night.

For weeks, she booked conventions, proms, reunions, wedding receptions, bar mitzvahs, and sweet-sixteen parties. She accepted reservations for the hotel's restaurant. Then she sat back and watched as the hotel was inundated by furious clients who insisted that they had booked rooms, or a table for dinner, or a ballroom for a special event. Of course, the hotel computer system had no record of any of these reservations. Soon the hotel filed for bankruptcy.

Then the woman's phone rang again. A representative from Marriott made an offer for the defunct hotel. "I'll take it," she said. "But only if you get a new telephone number for the hotel."

Age Has Its Advantages

An elderly woman drove her Mercedes into a shopping mall's crowded parking lot on a Saturday morning before Christmas. There were no spaces available, so she pulled to one side and waited. A shopper came out of the mall, saw the woman waiting.

"I'm leaving now," she said. "You can have my space."

The shopper loaded her purchases into her car's trunk and backed out. But before the woman in the Mercedes could park, a young man in a shiny red MG cut ahead of her and took the parking space. As he ran past toward the mall.

"Face it! I'm younger and faster!" he shouted as he ran toward the mall.

The woman was quiet for a moment. Then she backed up, hit the gas, and slammed into the MG. She backed up and did it again. And again. And again.

The young man ran back to his crumpled MG.

"What are you doing? Are you crazy?"

"Face it! I'm older and I have more insurance," the elderly woman said. Then she drove away.

The Bothered Bride

After dating for three years, Tony and Tina decided to get married. Tina's friends were not sure this was such a great idea—Tony had a well-earned reputation for being a babe-hound. He had strayed several times while dating Tina, yet she always forgave him. Once the engagement was announced, however, Tony was a changed man. He was attentive, considerate, and showed no signs of chasing other women. Everyone was relieved.

The wedding day came and it was perfect. It was the loveliest day in June. The bride was radiant. The groom was handsome.

At the reception, family members and friends competed with one another to give the funniest, sweetest toast to the happy couple. And after all the toasts were done, the bride stood up. This was unexpected, and everyone fell silent to hear what Tina had to say.

"First," she began, "I want to say how touched I am that all of my relatives and all of my friends are here with me today. You are very dear to me. "Next, I want to thank my mom and dad who gave me this beautiful wedding. You are the most important people in the world to me."

Everyone in the reception hall beamed as Tina's parents wiped tears from their eyes.

"Finally," Tina said, "I have a special wedding favor for all of my guests. Please reach underneath your chairs and open the envelope you'll find there."

The bride waited as all her guests opened the envelopes. Inside were photographs of Tony having sex with the maid of honor.

Then Tina turned to Tony.

"You sonofabitch! Did you really think I'd fall for all those lame excuses why you had to leave the apartment 'just for a couple of hours' every night for the past month? I knew you were cheating on me and I hired a private detective to find out who it was."

Tina picked up her bouquet, slapped the maid of honor across the face.

"You're a slut!" she cried. Then she slapped Tony. "And you're going to get the bill for this wedding," she said.

With that, Tina stomped out of the reception hall.

The Frat Boys' Peace-Offering

At the University of Wisconsin in Madison, a sorority house stood next door to a fraternity house. The sisters and brothers hung out and studied together on school nights and partied together on weekends. There was only one weekend of the year when relations between the sorority and the fraternity broke down—at the annual Men's Aggression Night it was guys only at the frat house.

Typically, the evening was a testosterone-fest of ear-shattering music, brawling in the street, and vomiting in the bushes, followed by deathly silence the next day as the boys tried to recover from their killer hangovers. But one year the party turned ugly. The frat boys directed all their aggression on the sorority house—brawling on their lawn, puking in their bushes, and even trying to break down the front door.

The sisters called the cops and about a dozen frat boys were hauled away for disorderly conduct.

About 9 a.m. the next morning, there was knock at the battered front door of the sorority house. There stood the officers and executive committee of the frat.

"We've come to apologize," the president said. "We were animals last night. We deserved to have the police shut us down. And even though twelve brothers spent the night in jail, we wanted to prove to you that there are no hard feelings."

At this, the president and the other officers handed over four boxes of donuts from the best bakery in town.

"Please accept this with out compliments," the frat president said. "You deserve it."

The sorority girls were very pleased with the boys' abject apology and the peace offering. They put on more coffee, and sat down to a breakfast of donuts.

The donuts were almost gone when one of the sorority sisters noticed a Polaroid at the bottom of one of the boxes.

"Omigod!" she shrieked. "Look at this."

The photo showed all the frat brothers, naked, and wearing donuts on the erect portion of their anatomies.

Extra Cheese

A high school boy in Milwaukee got a night job delivering pizza. It was decent work and most of his customer's were good tippers, but there was one address he hated going to. Half a mile from Marquette University was a house where 10 college guys all lived together. At least four times a week they ordered pizzas, and they always did something to make the delivery boy's life miserable.

Once, while he was at the door with the order, a couple of the guys let the air out of tires of his delivery truck. Another time, when the delivery boy brought 30 pizzas to the house for a party, the college guys took the pizzas and refused to pay.

After months of enduring their pranks and abuse, the delivery boy had had enough. One stormy night, he got a call to deliver a pizza with extra cheese to college guys' house. The rain was coming down in sheets and driving was hazardous, but the kid's boss insisted that he make the delivery. When he arrived at the door, the guys complained that this wasn't their order.

"We said 'extra cheese.' Take it back and bring us another pizza."

The delivery boy returned to the pizzeria, sprinkled another handful of mozzarella over the pizza, placed it back in the oven, and then went out in the storm again to make the delivery.

Again, the college guys complained that there wasn't enough cheese on the pizza. And once again the delivery boy went back to the pizzeria to add more cheese.

The next time he returned to the house, one of the guys said, "Well, it looks like it has extra cheese, but it doesn't have any string cheese. Take it back and put some string cheese on it."

The kid wanted to slug the idiot, but with 10 against one, he would have gotten the crap beaten out of him. So he climbed back into his truck and headed for the pizzeria. He didn't know what he was going to tell his boss. They didn't have string cheese at the pizzeria—it wasn't an ingredient people asked for. That's when the kid had an idea.

At the pizzeria he added even more mozzarella, popped the pizza back in the oven, then hurried out to the truck. When he was a couple of blocks from the house, he parked the truck and climbed into the back. It was dark and warm in there were no windows. Nobody could see him as he unzipped his jeans and began to rub his penis. When he felt that he was ready to shoot, he opened the pizza box and came all over the pizza. Then he closed the box and made the delivery.

The college kid who opened the door checked the pizza.

"Good. You added the string cheese. You even managed to get

it on every part of the pizza. Nice job, kid."

The Heiress' Revenge

There is an abandoned family graveyard near a burned out plantation in Georgia. All the graves are marked with conventional headstones and obelisks, except for one. Over that singular grave the family erected a life-size sculpture of a young woman, seated on a bench, her arms stretched out as if she were inviting someone to embrace her.

Local legend says this is the grave the heiress to the plantation. She had fallen in love with a dashing young man from Charleston named Morgan. He asked her to marry him. But the night before their wedding, Morgan came to see his fiance, and told her he could not marry her. His family would not give their consent, he said and they had already arranged for him to marry someone else. The poor jilted bride died of a broken heart.

It became a tradition among the sororities at a college near the graveyard that new pledges should spend the night sitting in the statue's lap—keeping company the sad, lonely woman.

One year, a freshman from Charleston pledged the sorority. The sisters told her the story of the jilted plantation heiress and her hardhearted lover, Morgan.

"What a coincidence," the new pledge said. "I'm from Charleston and my name is Morgan. I wonder if we're related."

On the final night of pledge week, the sisters took the new girl to the graveyard. They watched as she climbed onto the statue's lap.

"We'll see you in the morning," the president of the sorority said. Then the girls left the pledge alone.

Early the next morning all the sorority sisters returned to the graveyard with hot coffee and donuts to welcome their new sister. They could see that she was still sitting in the statue's lap, but she didn't respond to any of their calls. "She must have fallen asleep," one of the girls said. She strolled over to wake her new sister, but when she got to the statue she began to scream.

The new pledge was indeed still in the statue's lap. But the arms of the statue no longer reached out. Now they were wrapped tightly around the girl. On the dead girl's face was a look of terror. But the statue's old expression of sorrow had been replaced by a look of joy and triumph.

The heiress had avenged herself on the family of Morgan.

The Boyfriend's Revenge

Jenny and Marty met at orientation on the first day of high school and were inseparable for the next four years. Neither one ever dated anyone else, and they lost their virginity to each other on the night of their senior prom. They had planned to go to the same college and then get married, but there was one glitch. Jenny got into Boston College; Marty did not. Marty got into UCLA; Jenny did not. The disappointment almost broke the two lovers' hearts, but they promised each other to remain faithful.

At first Jenny and Marty spoke to each other on the phone every night and sent each other e-mail throughout the day. But as time went by Jenny started to get into Boston College's party scene. She especially liked the out-of-control frat house parties. Lots of the guys at these parties asked her out, and she was getting tired of saying no and spending her nights alone while her roommate and other new friends went out on dates.

Marty was so far away, and four years was such a long time—Jenny began to think that she had been an idiot to promise to remain monogamous all though college.

Meanwhile, Marty was running into lots of temptations himself. Southern California was full of beautiful girls. His roommate and his new friends thought he was out of his mind to pass up so many opportunities for a good time. But Marty was determined to stay faithful to Jenny. Since he had to do something with his sexual energy, he put it all into his schoolwork and became a straight-A student for the first time in his life.

Jenny, on the other hand, had decided to take advantage of her opportunities. At the next frat party a handsome junior, a member of the college's hockey team, asked her out and she accepted. At the end of the evening, Jenny went back to the hockey player's room and spent the night with him.

The next morning she felt guilty. She decided the best thing to do was break it off with Marty. So she sent him an e-mail saying their relationship was over, that she was dating someone else and he should, too.

Marty was stunned. He couldn't believe it. He called Jenny, but she wouldn't speak to him. He sent e-mails that he would wait for her. She sent emails back saying he shouldn't. It would be pointless. It was over.

Marty was certain once they saw each other at Christmas they would be together again. He kept pestering Jenny with phone calls, letters, e-mails, faxes, flowers, candy, teddy bears and Mylar balloons. Jenny could see that Marty was going to go away quietly.

She had an idea. Jenny asked her roommate to photograph her making love to the hockey player. Jenny's boyfriend said it was fine with him! In fact, he really liked the idea.

The next day, Jenny sent the photographs to Marty with a note that read: "Marty—I have a new boyfriend. Get lost."

At first Marty was crushed. Then he was angry. Finally, he decided to get even. He took out a piece of stationary.

"Dear Mom and Dad, College is so wonderful! I'm having a great time! But my sheets are wearing out. Please send money so I can buy more. Love, Jenny," he wrote.

Marty put the note and photographs into an envelope and sent it that day to Jenny's parents.

"He's Not Much of a Man"

A trucker stopped at an all-night diner in the Ozarks. He ordered a couple of hamburgers, a large plate of French fries, and a cup of coffee. Soon after his food arrived, two redneck kids roared up to the diner on motorcycles. They walked inside and sat down at the counter next to the trucker, one on either side.

They ate one of the man's burgers, grabbed handfuls of fries off his plate and drank his coffee. Through all this, the trucker did not say a word. He ate what the boys had not touched, left a tip, paid his bill, and walked out of the diner.

"He's not much of a man, is he?" one of the rednecks said to the guy behind the counter.

"And he's not much of a driver either," the counterman said. "He just ran his truck over your bikes."

Rough Justice

A lawyer found that she had left at home a file she would need at her afternoon meeting. During lunch she drove back to her house and she was surprised to see her husband's car in the driveway. As she stepped into the kitchen, she could hear the sounds of a man and a woman making love in the family room. The lawyer took off her shoes and tiptoed to the doorway. There on the floor in front of the fireplace was her husband making love to his secretary.

Without making a sound, the woman returned to kitchen picked up the file she needed from the counter, and drove back to the office. She called her mother and asked her to pick up the kids after school and let them stay at her place that night.

That evening the woman stopped at the fish market and bought two lobsters and two dozen raw oysters. At the wine shop she picked up a bottle of Dom Perignon. Once she was home, she set the table, lit the candles, chilled the champagne, put the oysters on ice, and boiled the lobster. Her husband was delighted to find his wife had prepared a romantic evening just for the two of them.

After the meal, the woman put on her sexiest underwear and slipped into bed beside her husband. Soon he was fully aroused, but his wife insisted that he wait a little longer.

"I have one last surprise for you," she whispered.

As she took a small tube from her nightstand, the husband asked, "Have you found some sexy new lubricant?"

"Yeah," his wife said. "Something like that. Just wait."

The woman squeezed the liquid from the tube onto her husband's belly and then pressed his erect penis against it.

"It's cold and sticky," he said. "What's this stuff called?"

"It's called Super Glue," she said. "Now while you call the ambulance, I'm going to get my cell phone and call a divorce lawyer."

Call Waiting

A man and a woman had been living together for two years. The woman expected they would get married, but the guy was bored with his girlfriend. He wanted to be single again.

"I'm sorry to say this, but I don't want to live with you anymore. I want to see other women. And since this is my apartment, I'm afraid I'll have to ask you to move out. I know it sounds cruel, but I want all of your things out of here by the time I get back two weeks from now," the guy told his girlfriend the morning he was leaving on a two-week business trip.

The poor woman was stunned. She just stared and couldn't say a word. The man picked up his briefcase and his luggage.

"This is good-bye," he said.

During the two weeks he was traveling, the guy had to admit that he had been harsh.

"It's better this way," he told himself. "At least I was honest."

He was worried, however, that when he returned home his apartment would be trashed, or his girlfriend would still be there and refused to leave. Given a choice, he would prefer a trashed apartment.

The two weeks passed and the man returned home. He took a deep breath and then opened his apartment door. Everything looked fine. It fact, the place was immaculate. His girlfriend had cleaned before she left. As he wandered from room to room, he found no trace of her. She had taken everything that was hers and nothing that was his.

Then the man heard a strange sound. He traced in to the bedroom where he found the telephone off the hook and gibberish coming from the speaker. The man put the phone back on its base and then, just to be certain it was in working order, he called his best friend. The call went through with no trouble. He never gave the phone being off the hook another thought.

A week later his telephone bill arrived. On it were charges for a call to the time and weather information number in Beijing, China. According to the bill, the call had been made the day he left on his business trip and had continued uninterrupted for the next two weeks until the day he returned and put the phone back on the hook. The charge for the 14-day long distance phone call was $75,000.

The Vigilante Grandmother

An 81-year-old grandmother in Sydney, Australia, was very upset when her granddaughter's latest boyfriend hit the girl and gave her a black eye.

"Stop seeing him," the grandmother said. "Anyone who does this to you is an animal. Get rid of him now."

The girl wouldn't listen, so the grandmother decided to speak to the boyfriend.

"If you ever touch my granddaughter again. I am going to make you very sorry," she said.

The boy smirked.

"Yeah. Sure. No problem, Granny. By the way, you really scare me," he said.

"Just remember what I said," the grandmother replied.

Although the boyfriend no longer hit the girl, he took every opportunity to humiliate her in public. He shouted obscenities at her in restaurants and movie theaters, insulted her and belittled her in front of his friends. After several months of this, the girlfriend had had enough and broke up with the slob. Her grandmother was greatly relieved.

Late one night a week after the break-up, the girl was walking home from a friend's house when she saw her ex-boyfriend and one of his friends leaning against a lamp post at the corner. She turned around and began walking back to her friend's house, but the two young men ran after her, caught her and dragged her into an alley where they raped the poor girl.

The grandmother was heartbroken when she heard what had happened to her granddaughter. She hurried to the hospital to see the poor girl.

"Have the police arrested them yet?" she asked.

"No," the girl answered. "I told the police I didn't know who the men were and I couldn't give a description because it was too dark to see their faces."

The grandmother was stunned.

"Dear child, why did you say such a thing?"

"They said they would kill me if I turned them in," the girl answered. Then she began to cry.

The grandmother kissed her granddaughter and left the hospital. She stopped at her house to get something from her late husband's room, then she climbed back into her car and began driving around town. She drove to every place her granddaughter had ever mentioned going with her ex-boyfriend. At last she found him and his friend on a rotting wharf down by the harbor.

The guys laughed when they saw an 81-year-old woman walking toward them carrying a shotgun.

"I said you would be sorry if you ever hurt my granddaughter," the old woman said.

"What are you gonna do, Granny," the boyfriend said. "You gonna kill us?"

"No. I'm going to make sure you never hurt another girl again." Then the grandmother raised the shotgun and shot both boys in the groin.

The Innkeeper's Revenge

A little boy had been cast as St. Joseph in his parish's Christmas pageant. He was a cute little guy, but he couldn't remember his lines. After four weeks of rehearsal and with the date of the pageant only three days away, the boy still couldn't get his lines right.

Reluctantly, the nun who was directing the pageant gave the boy the part of the innkeeper, a role with only one line, and promoted the innkeeper to the part of St. Joseph.

The original St. Joseph was not happy about being demoted. "It's your own fault," his rival said. "You should have studied your lines like Sister said. Now I'm the star of the show, and you're a nobody."

This observation did sit well.

Nonetheless, at dress rehearsal the new innkeeper recited his one line perfectly and gave no sign of resentment. The nun still felt bad about making the switch, but at least the boy had taken it well.

The next night the church hall was packed with parents and relatives. The nun was pleased that all the children were remembering their lines. Then came the scene in which Mary and Joseph meet the innkeeper.

The boy playing Joseph recited his line.

"Master Innkeeper, do you have a room for me and my wife Mary. She's about to have a baby."

The innkeeper glared at Joseph. "I have a deluxe room for Mary," he said, "but you can go to hell!"

Cheating Stinks

A woman and her boyfriend had bought a beautiful house together overlooking the Long Island Sound. One day she came home from work early to find her boyfriend in bed with another woman. Much as she would have liked to start a brawl, the jilted girlfriend kept her self-control.

"I'll be back tomorrow to clean out my stuff. I don't want to find either one of you here," she said.

The next day the woman returned to the house with a couple of friends and began packing up her things. While her helpers carried the last boxes out to the moving truck, the woman went into the master bedroom with a shopping bag. She took down the shiny brass curtain rod over the bedroom window and unscrewed one of the finals. From the shopping bag she took a half dozen jumbo shrimp, stuffed them into the hollow rod, screwed the finial on again, hung the rod over the window, and left the house.

The next morning, the new girlfriend complained that something smelled odd in the bedroom. So the man took all his dirty clothes down to the basement and threw them in the washer.

But the smell persisted.

The couple sent all the bedding and the Oriental carpets to the dry cleaner. They bought new pillows. They scrubbed down the walls, ceiling and floor. They hung air fresheners throughout the room. They burned incense.

Still, the smell persisted. In fact, it got worse.

"Maybe a mouse died inside the walls or under the floor," the man suggested. So he tore down the bedroom walls and ripped up the floor. But he found nothing. And the stench was getting worse.

Now it was July and the couple couldn't bear to go into the master bedroom. They slept in the guest room on the first floor, but the stink had invaded every room of the house. In desperation, they put the house up for sale.

The old girlfriend heard that her ex and his new girlfriend had bought a new house together. On moving day the old girlfriend sat in her car at the end of the block and watched the movers carry furniture and boxes into the moving truck. She sat and watched for three hours, and she only drove away when she saw the movers place the brass curtain rod in the truck.

WAITING FOR THE ICEMAN AND OTHER SEXUAL ESCAPADES

WAITING FOR THE ICEMAN

Back at the turn of the 20th century, a woman was about to step into the bath tub when she realized that she had forgotten to leave the back door open for the ice man.

Without even putting on her bathrobe, she raced downstairs to the kitchen and threw open the back door. Standing on the back porch was her next door neighbor.

The naked woman froze. The man stared.

"My wife sent me over to borrow a couple of eggs," he finally managed to stammer.

"Oh," said the naked woman. "Well, I was just waiting for the iceman."

She Found Her Thrill on Hyde Street Hill

A 23-year-old woman from Holland, Michigan, traveled to San Francisco to visit her cousin. It was her first trip to the City by the Bay and she enjoyed doing all the typical tourist things. But she could not get enough of riding the cable cars. She tried to plan her sightseeing around the cable car routes, and even then she often concluded her day with a few extra trips up and down the hills of

San Francisco.

On her fifth day in the city, she was taking a cable car up Hyde Street when the car lost its grip and began to plunge backward down the hill. The young woman was thrown to the back to car. When the police and paramedics arrived, they found the Michigan tourist unconscious, with two black eyes, some serious bruises, and her legs wrapped around an upright pole at the rear of the car.

Her cousin was at her bedside when the Michigan tourist regained consciousness.

"I feel so strange," the woman said.

"Of course you do, honey," her cousin said. "You were in a nasty accident. All those bruises. And two black eyes. It must be painful. Do you want me to call a nurse to give you a pain killer?"

"No, I really don't feel that much pain. What I do feel is incredibly horny," she said.

Poor girl, her cousin thought. She's delirious from the accident.

But delirium, like the bruises, was not the Michigan tourist's problem. Her trouble was her libido. Something happened during the accident that set her G-spot on overdrive and now she could barely control herself. Throughout her hospital stay, she tried to seduce every man who walked into her room. Doctors. Orderlies. Male nurses. Hospital administrators. She even lured into her room men who had come to the hospital to visit other patients. She was very insistent, and some of the men were only too happy to respond.

The woman's attending physician was perplexed. The cousin told him that the woman had had several relationships in the past few years, but she had always been discrete. So the doctor called for a psychiatric consultation.

The psychiatrist's diagnosis was nymphomania.

"I don't know why a cable car accident would set off nymphomania," the psychiatrist said. "But this is a textbook case nonetheless."

Once she was released from the hospital, the woman gave her new insatiable appetite full rein. She moved out of her cousin's apartment and into a hotel, but the hotel management suspected that any woman who saw men in that volume had to be a prostitute. They asked her to leave.

The poor woman's appetite was still insatiable, but now she was ashamed. She knew that something strange had come happened, that she needed professional help, and she suspected that it would be expensive. So she sued the cable car company.

In court, several San Francisco psychiatrists testified the woman did indeed suffer from nymphomania, that it dated from the cable car accident and the condition was destroying her life. The jury—eight women and four men—was sympathetic. They awarded the woman $1 million. And all four male jurors offered to take her out for a celebration dinner.

A Boy's Best Friend

A 15-year-old boy was playing with himself in his bedroom when he heard his mother calling him.

"Your grandparents are coming over for dinner tonight," she said. "I have to go to the supermarket. While I'm gone, you can vacuum the house."

The kid started to whine, but his mother pretended not to notice.

"I'll be back in an hour and a half. That will give you more than enough time. And use the new vacuum." Then she walked out the door.

The boy moped around for ten minutes or so, then he went to the utility closet and took out the new vacuum cleaner. His mother had just spent $500 on this deluxe model. The suction was supposed to be strong enough to lift a bowling ball, but since no one in the family bowled they weren't able to test it.

The kid vacuumed the kitchen, the dining room and the living room. Then he went back to the closet to get the attachments to vacuum the furniture. There was a long flexible vinyl hose with a soft brush at the end. He ran the bristles over his arm, they gave him goosebumps. He placed his hand over the hose and felt the force of suction. That's when he had an idea.

He locked the front and back doors, dragged the machine to a windowless corner of the living room, and unzipped his pants. He slipped his penis into the hose and turned the vacuum on low. The sensation was electric. He had never known anything that felt so wonderful. It didn't take long before he came.

He went back to vacuuming the furniture, but his mind was on his last orgasm. The thought of it got him excited and soon he was ready again. Once more he unzipped his pants, slid his penis inside the hose, and this time put the setting on medium. It was as if every nerve in his body had caught fire. A few moments later he dropped to his knees from the intensity of the most explosive orgasm of his life.

Afterward, the kid lay on the living room floor. All thought of going back to housekeeping had vanished. He was just giving himself enough time to recover so he could experience the ultimate— the vacuum cleaner set on high.

He remained flat on his back as he slipped the hose over his penis, then reached over, turned the vacuum's setting up, and hit the ON button. The boy almost blacked out from the force of the suction, but within moments the pleasure had changed to excruciating pain. He curled into the fetal position and cried out in agony— he felt as if the vacuum cleaner would rip his penis off. He reached for the OFF button and knocked the vacuum over instead. He was screaming from the pain as he dragged himself across the floor and hit the OFF button.

He wept tears of relief as the vacuum fell silent and the suction stopped. Afraid of what he would see, he closed his eyes and slowly, gently, slid the hose off his penis. Wave after wave of agony came over him. When at last he did open his eyes, he began to wail. His penis was raw and bruised—and stretched 20-inches long.

The Girl Who Loved Her Cat

The game show version of this classic urban legend first started circulating in 1999.

A game show in Puerto Rico ran a contest in which first prize was a chance to meet the Latin pop superstar Ricky Martin. The parents of a 15-year-old girl, who was a huge Ricky Martin fan, entered her name in the contest and won!

While the girl was at school, a camera crew from the game show came to the family's home, placed tiny cameras discreetly throughout the house, hid Ricky Martin in the girl's bedroom closet, and took the parents back to the studio so they could witness their daughter's surprise with millions of other viewers.

A few moments after the game show went on the air, the girl came home from school. The cameras caught her every movement. She dropped her school books on the kitchen table, opened the refrigerator, and took out a can of paté. With the paté, she walked through the house and upstairs to her bedroom. The cameras in her room recorded her as she stood before a full-length mirror and stripped off all her clothes. Then she spread the paté on her erogenous zones, lay down on her bed, and called the family cat. The animal raced into the bedroom, leapt onto the bed, and began nibbling at the paté while the girl moaned with pleasure.

Meanwhile, the girl's parents had left the studio in shame. They never saw Ricky Martin step out of the closet. He took one look at the naked girl, the paté, and the cat.

"Well, I guess you don't need me," he said.

Variant: The classic version of this urban legend tells of a young woman who smeared peanut butter on her private parts and let her dog lick it off. She was discovered in the act by her fiancee, family, and friends who had hidden in her apartment to throw her a surprise party.

The Blind Man

This story originated in New Zealand in the 1950s.

A woman had just undressed and was about to step into the shower when she heard the doorbell ring.

"Who is it?" she shouted from the bathroom window.

"Blind man," a man answered.

The woman sighed. It was too much trouble to get dressed again, so she thought she would just run downstairs and give the poor man some money as she was.

"There's nothing to be ashamed of," she told herself. "He can't see a thing."

The naked woman grabbed a few dollars from her purse and threw open the door.

The man on the back porch gasped. Then he smiled. "Good morning, ma'am," he said. "Where would you like me to hang the blinds?"

The Amazing Breath Freshener

Two marketing executives, Sally and Victoria, were having lunch. "I saw that huge flower arrangement in your office," Sally said. "Why is your boyfriend apologizing? How did he screw up?"

"Actually," Victoria said, "those aren't 'Forgive me' flowers; those are "Thank you, you were fantastic flowers."

Sally leaned across the table, "What did you do, girl?"

Victoria glanced around at the neighboring tables to make sure no one was close enough to hear.

"Okay. Last night Michael and I went out to dinner and then I wound up back at his place. I didn't have my toothbrush with me, so before we went to bed, I chewed four Altoids."

"You mean those really obnoxious mints?"

"Exactly. Well, I had had a few glasses of wine at dinner and I found myself doing what Michael has always asked me to do."

"Oral sex?!"

"Uh huh. And he says it was amazing. He was literally screaming. And this morning he left this steamy message on my voice mail calling me the oral goddess. Thank God I didn't have it set on speaker phone."

"And you think the Altoids made the difference?" Sally said.

"Honey," Victoria said, "buy a box and try it tonight yourself. The mints have this lasting tingling sensation, it drove Michael wild."

And Sally did that just that. The next morning she had a huge, gorgeous bouquet of flowers on her desk from her husband. She told two or three select friends why, and they told a few of their friends in the office. At lunch time, the women and gay men in the office were stampeding to drug stores and newspaper stands to buy Altoids. And the straight guys in the office were trying to figure out how they could get their wives and girlfriends to chew a few Altoids before sex.

Meanwhile, Victoria was on the phone to her broker. "Get me 1000 shares of Altoid's stock," she told him. "It's going to be bigger than Viagra."

You Can't Fool the Doctor

A tall, blond-haired, blue-eyed farmer's son from Iowa went to college in San Francisco. His freshman year his roommate was gay. This didn't bother the Iowa boy at all.

"He's never even made a pass at me, so why should I care what he does?" he told his straight friends.

But after a few weeks at college, the Iowa boy found himself suffering from chronic anal pain. He assumed its was hemorrhoids, but none of the over-the-counter creams gave him any relief.

After two months of suffering he made an appointment with a doctor at the college's clinic. After the doctor finished examining the boy he said, "You'll feel a lot better if you cut out the rough anal sex."

"What are you talking about?" the Iowa boy said. "I'm not gay! I've never had anal sex in my life!"

"Look, son," the doctor said, "you can mislead your folks, and you can mislead your friends, but you can't fool your doctor."

The Iowa kid left the clinic upset and confused. When he got back to his room, he found a note from his roommate saying, "I'm going home for the weekend. See you Monday."

That's when the Iowa boy got an idea. He started searching through his roommate's closet, his bureau, his desk. But he didn't find anything suspicious until he looked under his roommate's bed.

There he discovered a plastic bag full of terry cloth hand towels, a jar of K-Y jelly, a large dildo, and a can of ether.

The Iowa boy reported his roommate to the dean, got him expelled, and enjoyed the luxury of a dorm room all to himself for the rest of his freshman year.

What Grows to Six Times Its Normal Size?

The biology instructor at a small college in Virginia was reviewing material for his class' upcoming midterm. "Miss Spencer," he said, "under proper conditions a certain organ of the human body expands to six times its normal size. Name the organ and the necessary conditions for its expansion."

The young woman was silent for a moment. Then she said, "Professor, that is an indecent question. We have not covered any material on human reproduction. And I am going to file complaint of sexual harassment with the dean." Miss Spencer collected her books and was beginning to walk out of the room when the Professor stopped her.

"Before you leave, Miss Spencer, you should know that the correct answer is the pupil of the eye which expands to six times its normal size in dim light."

"I think if any one has a dirty mind, Miss Spencer," the professor said, "it's you. And by the way, when you do get around to experiencing human reproduction, I'm afraid that you're in for a big disappointment."

The Stamp Dispenser

A woman had an appointment with her gynecologist. When she arrived at his office the receptionist said the doctor was running late. After half an hour, the woman left the waiting room and went down the hall to the ladies room.

When she finished, she found that there was no toilet paper in her stall. So she used some tissues she had in her purse. What she didn't know was a strip of postage stamps was stuck to the tissue and when she wiped herself they transferred to her private parts.

A few minutes after she returned to the waiting room, the doctor was finally ready to see her.

The woman climbed up on the table and the gynecologist began the examination. Very gently he removed the stamps, held them up for his patient to see.

"That's a very interesting stamp dispenser you have, Mrs. Wilson!" he said.

The License

A newlywed couple spent their honeymoon in Mexico. One afternoon they went to the hotel's exchange desk to buy pesos, but the hotel had run out.

"There is a cash machine at a bank two blocks from here that accepts American ATM cards," the desk clerk said.

While the husband ran off to the bank, the wife waited in front of the hotel. But there was a long line at the ATM. A five-minute errand took more than half an hour. Meanwhile, the young woman was pacing impatiently back and forth in front of the hotel.

Then a police officer approached the woman. "Business is slow today."

"Excuse me?" she said.

"No customers," the policeman said. "I have been watching you for the last 30 minutes."

"I don't know what you're talking about," the woman said.

"You American streetwalkers are so obvious. Don't you know better than to be try to solicit customers right in front of a fine resort hotel? I must write you a summons."

"Streetwalker! I'm waiting for my husband. He went to the bank."

At that moment the husband arrived and assured the police officer he had made a terrible mistake.

"It is too late, señor," the policeman said. "I have already written the summons. Your wife must appear in court to answer a charge of soliciting."

"But isn't there another solution?" the husband said. "Can't we just pay a fine instead of going to court?"

"A fine, no," the policeman said. "But I can issue you a license."

"I don't understand," the woman said.

"Streetwalking is not illegal here," the policeman said. "Just unlicensed streetwalking. For 25 pesos the lady will be licensed by the city of Cancun to conduct her business anywhere she chooses."

"And we can get this license now?" the husband said. "We don't have to go to court?"

"Absolutely," the policeman said.

"Then here's the 25 pesos," the husband said.

When the newlyweds returned home, they had the wife's streetwalking license framed and hung it in their bedroom.

The Amorous Dentist

A dentist in Detroit had a strange fetish. Whenever an attractive woman came to him for an examination, he told her she had a bad tooth that would require very painful drilling. He urged the patient, for her own sake, to let him put her under with anesthesia so she wouldn't feel the pain of the procedure. Then, while the woman was asleep, the dentist had sex with her inert body.

The dentist had been doing this for a couple of years when one day an underwear model came to his office. One of her fillings had fallen out and she was in a lot of pain.

Having sex with a model was a fantasy come true for the dentist. But in his excitement, he didn't use as much anesthesia as usual. The woman woke up while he was on top of her. She pressed charges and the story was picked up by newspapers and entertainment magazines.

After a brief trial, the dentist was found guilty. The headline for the story that ran in Entertainment Weekly read, "Dentist convicted of filling wrong cavity."

The Misunderstood Note

At a sexual assault trial, the victim, a young woman, barely 18 years old, could not bring herself to repeat on the stand what the rapist had said to her.

"I won't force you, Miss," the judge told her. "Just write down what he said on this slip of paper and I'll pass it along to the jury."

The woman took the paper and pen from the judge and wrote, "I want to f**k you until you die."

The judge read the note, then directed the bailiff to give it to the foreman of the jury. The jurors passed the note silently among themselves. Finally a woman handed the note to the last juror, a man who had dosed off during the proceedings. She shook him awake and gave him the paper.

He read it, smiled at the woman juror, and stuck the note in his pocket.

"Sir, you must give that paper to me," the judge told the man.

"I don't think so, judge," the man answered. "This is a private note from this lady here to me."

The Policeman's Ball

A very beautiful young woman was driving her sports car more than 90 miles per hour down a highway in Tennessee when a state trooper pulled her over.

She gave the police officer her most dazzling smile, apologized in the most earnest manner and even shed a few tears. But to all of these ploys, the state trooper was unmoved. He just kept writing out the ticket.

Finally, the young lady tried a different approach.

"Please, officer, my husband will have a fit if I come home with a speeding ticket. Could you forget about this incident if bought a few tickets for the policemen's ball?"

The state trooper stopped writing, looked the young woman in the eye.

"Ma'am, I'm a state trooper. State policeman don't have balls," he said.

The young woman was silent for a moment.

"From the way you look, I never would have guessed," she said.

The cop blushed deep red, tore up the ticket and walked back to his car.

The Cheating Wife

A man knew his wife was having an affair. When she announced that she was pregnant, the husband disowned the baby.

The wife's boyfriend also refused any responsibility for the child. So the woman did the only thing she could do: wait.

Six months later the woman gave birth to twin boys. To determine paternity, she demanded a blood test.

A few hours later, her obstetrician returned to the new mother's room with the results of the blood test.

"In twenty years of medical practice, I've never even heard of such a thing," he said. "One of your babies was fathered by your husband. The other twin was fathered by your boyfriend. Lady, you've just hit the child support jackpot."

The Tell-tale Condom

A gynecologist was out playing golf with a long-time friend. After 18 holes, they went to the club house for a couple of drinks. Halfway through the third martini the gynecologist got talkative.

"You know," he said to his friend, "your wife came to see me the other day."

"She comes to see you all the time," the other golfer said. "You're her doctor."

"Yes, but this time the examination has something to do with you," the doctor said. Then he took a deep breath. "I'm probably in breech of medical ethics, but we've been friends for years and your wife's health is involved."

"Now you've got me nervous," the doctor's friend said. "What did you find?"

"Well, during the examination, I removed a used condom that was stuck inside your wife. I'm sorry if I'm intruding on your privacy, but you just can't do that type of thing. The impact it could have your wife's health is staggering."

The gynecologist could tell that his friend was furious.

"Look, I'm not being critical, I'm just urging you to be more careful next time," he said.

"You don't get it," his friend said. "I'm not angry with you. I'm furious with my wife."

"You can't blame her for this," the gynecologist said.

"Oh yes I can. In fifteen years of making love to that woman, I've never used a condom!"

Caught in the Act

Two sixteen-year-old sweethearts were delighted when their parents agreed that the two families would go camping together in Wyoming. The camp site the families chose was perfect with spectacular views of the mountains, a beautiful forest and, just a couple hundred yards from the camp site, a lovely waterfall.

After three days in paradise, the young couple decided this was the perfect place to consummate their love. One afternoon, after telling their parents they were going for a hike, the boy and girl slipped away to the waterfall and made love. But their passion made them lose all sense of time.

When five hours had passed and the young couple still had not returned to the camp site, their parents went looking for them. Eventually they found their children at the waterfall, lying together on a large flat rock, naked, the boy on top of the girl.

Panicked at the sight of her parents, the girl experienced a bizarre physiological reaction: her pelvis muscles locked. The boy couldn't withdraw, the girl couldn't release him. Everything the parents said or did to help only increased the girl's humiliation. Her pelvic muscles clamped tighter and tighter.

By the time the ambulance crew finally reached the waterfall, the girl was weeping with shame and the boy was screaming in agony.

The Substitute

A 20-year-old American sailor had shore leave in Singapore. While he was having a few drinks in a bar, an elderly, well-dressed man approached him.

"You are from the United States?" the old man asked. "How long will your ship be in port?"

"The captain says we'll be here a week," the sailor said.

"Perhaps," the old man said, "you would like some female company while you are in Singapore?"

"Absolutely!" the sailor said. "How much?"

"There is no charge. Consider it a gesture of friendship. Come with me."

The sailor was suspicious, but he decided to go along. Outside the bar, a black stretch limousine was waiting for the elderly gentleman. The driver took them to a magnificent villa on a hill high above the harbor.

"This is my home," the old man explained.

Inside, the sailor could scarcely believe his eyes. No cat house he had ever seen was so richly furnished. Fine paintings hung on the walls, every room was furnished with antiques. The old man led the sailor upstairs to a large bedroom where a beautiful young woman was waiting.

"I will call for you in the morning in time for you to return to your ship," the old man said. Then he closed the bedroom door.

The sailor and the beautiful woman made love all night long. Before sunrise, the limo took him back to his ship.

That evening, when the sailor went ashore again, the limo was waiting for him on the dock, along with a written invitation from the old man to visit the young woman again.

Every night for the next six nights, the pattern was repeated. As he climbed into the limo to be taken back to his ship for the last time, the driver handed the sailor an envelope. Inside was a letter from the old man.

"As you must have guessed by now, I am a wealthy man. None of my relatives are worthy to be my heirs, but I am too old to father a child. You have been my substitute. Already my beautiful young wife fills certain she has conceived by you. Please accept this small gift as a token of our gratitude."

Attached to the bottom of the letter was a check for $1 million.

The Cyberlover

Emily, a freshman at an all-women's college in western Massachusetts, missed her boyfriend. One dull Saturday night she logged onto a cybersex chat room. There she met the usual number of giggly 13-year-old boys and 60-year-old perverts. But there was one guy, RealMan4U, who seemed mature, experienced, and romantic.

After their first meeting in the chat room, Emily and RealMan4U met each other online every night for long conversations. By the second week, Emily wanted to see RealMan4U in the flesh.

"Let's hook up tomorrow night," she said.

"Can you get to Boston?" RealMan4U answered.

"Sure. It's a little over an hour's drive."

RealMan4U sent a message back.

"Excellent. Meet me at the Boylston Street Coffee Shop. I'll sit at the end of the bar. And I'll be wearing a yellow cotton sweater."

The next night Emily borrowed a friend's car and drove to Boston. Her heart was racing as she walked to the coffee shop. At the door, she took a deep breath, then stepped inside.

At the end of the bar sat a good looking older man in a yellow cotton sweater. The man turned toward the door as she walked in.

"Emily!"

"Daddy!"

The Gravy Ladle

Not long after a guy named Jack graduated from college he rented an apartment with a young woman named Ann Marie. Once the place was cleaned and painted, Jack invited his mother over for dinner.

Jack's mom had been suspicious about her son's living arrangements, but now that she saw Jack and Ann Marie together she was pretty sure that they were lovers.

At one point, when Ann Marie was in the kitchen, Jack said to his mother, "Look, Mom, I know what you're thinking. But you've got it all wrong. Ann Marie and I are just roommates. This is the only way either one of us can afford to pay the rent."

"Did I say a word?" his mother asked.

So Jack dropped the subject. The three of them had a nice meal, Jack's mom helped with the dishes, and then she went home.

A week later, Ann Marie asked Jack, "What did you do with the silver gravy ladle?"

"What are you talking about?"

"I used my grandmother's silver gravy ladle when your mother came for dinner last week," Ann Marie said. "Now I can't find it."

"You're not suggesting my mother swiped a gravy ladle?"

"No. Of course not. But maybe she put it away somewhere."

"To set your mind at ease," Jack said, "I'll e-mail my mom."

Jack went to the computer and sent his mother an e-mail.

"Mom, do remember what happened to the silver gravy ladle Ann Marie brought to the table last week? I'm not saying you have it and I'm not saying you don't, but Ann Marie can't find it."

A few hours later, Jack's mother e-mailed back.

"Jack, I'm not saying you do sleep with Ann Marie and I'm not saying you don't. But if Ann Marie really sleeps in her own bed, by now she would have found the gravy ladle."

The Specimen

A college boy had biology lab at 8 a.m. One day the professor announced that he would be conducting an experiment personally and he needed some volunteers.

"I'm going to scrape the inside of each volunteer's cheek, analyze the scrapings and then tell each of them what they ate during the past 12 hours," he said.

Three students volunteered, two girls and boy.

After studying the scrapings from the first girl the professor reported that he had found evidence of pizza, potato chips, toasted bagel, coffee, and mouthwash.

"That's right!" the first volunteer said. "You didn't miss a thing!"

The scrapings from the second girl's mouth showed traces of spinach salad, grapefruit, dry toast, and coffee.

"Yes!" the second girl said. "I'm dieting for Spring Break."

Finally the professor studied the scrapings from the boy's mouth. After a few minutes he glanced up from the microscope and gave the boy a strange look.

"What's matter, professor?"

The professor didn't answer but went back to studying the specimen.

"I can't make a definite reading," the professor said.

"Come on, professor," the boy said. "You can at least make an educated guess."

"Yeah," another guy in the class said. "Tell us what he's put his mouth over the last 12 hours!"

"You insist?" the professor asked his volunteer.

"Absolutely. I've got nothing to hide," the student said.

"Very well. My analysis shows traces of pizza. I've also found evidence of beer. And there's one more thing I've found in the scraping taken from your mouth," the professor said. "Sperm."

The Blind Date

A 19-year-old kid home from college for the summer was feeling lonely, so his best friend decided to fix him up with a blind date.

"This girl's a sure thing," the friend said. "I've spent a few wild nights with her myself, so when you pick her up tonight, make sure you're prepared."

That afternoon, the college boy went to the drug store to buy some condoms. To his dismay, he saw the condoms were kept on a shelf behind the pharmacist's counter. He would have to go up and ask for them. But every time he approached the counter, there was some sweet old lady there, or a young mother with small children.

After loitering around the store for half an hour, the pharmacist called to the boy.

"Young man, would step back here please?" In the storage room, out of sight of the other customers, the pharmacist held out a box of condoms. "Is this what you're looking for?" he said.

"How did you know?" the college kid said.

"Hey, I was young once," the pharmacist said. "I remember how embarrassing it was to have to walk into a drug store and ask for rubbers. So you've got a hot date tonight?"

"Yeah," said the relieved college kid. "She's supposed to be pretty hot. All the guys in town say she's a sure thing."

"Enjoy yourself, son," the pharmacist said. "And I'm glad you're being careful. Now get out of here and go rest up for your date."

At 8 p.m. the boy stood on the front porch of his date's house and rang the doorbell. But when the door opened and the kid saw his date's father, he vaulted over the porch railing and ran for his car.

It was the pharmacist.

Fun with Gerbils

David and Zander, a gay couple, heard of a famous movie star who had had the orgasm of a lifetime when his partner slipped a live gerbil up his anus. They decided to try it themselves.

On the appointed night, David pushed a cardboard toilet paper tube up Zander's rectum and then slipped in a gerbil they had bought at a pet shop that morning. In a few moments, Zander was shouting, "Enough! Enough! I can't take any more!"

David tried to grab the gerbil, but the critter was out of reach. Thinking the gerbil might be attracted by light, David struck a match and held it to the opening of the toilet paper tube. The flame ignited a pocket of gas inside Zander's colon and a small fireball shot out of the tube, severely burning David's face and setting his hair on fire.

The fireball also set fire to the gerbil's fur. It burrowed deeper into Zander's colon. Unfortunately, the gerbil ignited another, larger pocket of gas which shot the little creature out of the tube, straight into David's face. The gerbil's velocity broke David's nose.

At the hospital, David and Zander were treated for first and second degree burns. But the gerbil didn't make it.